'I have far more respect for the person with a single idea who gets there than for the person with a thousand ideas who does nothing' Thomas Edison

# DRAGONS' DEN **YOUR IDEA CAN MAKE YOU RICH**

DRAGONS' DEN
# YOUR IDEA CAN MAKE YOU RICH

Vermilion

1 3 5 7 9 10 8 6 4 2

Text © Vermilion 2005
Photography © BBCW 2005
Foreword © Evan Davis 2005

First published in the United Kingdom in 2005 by Vermilion, an imprint of Ebury Publishing

Random House UK Ltd.
Random House
20 Vauxhall Bridge Road
London SW1V 2SA

Random House Australia (Pty) Limited
20 Alfred Street, Milsons Point, Sydney,
New South Wales 2061, Australia

Random House New Zealand Limited
18 Poland Road, Glenfield,
Auckland 10, New Zealand

Random House (Pty) Limited
Endulini, 5A Jubilee Road, Parktown 2193, South Africa

Random House UK Limited Reg. No. 954009
www.randomhouse.co.uk

Papers used by Vermilion are natural, recyclable products made from wood grown in sustainable forests.

A CIP catalogue record is available for this book from the British Library.

ISBN: 0091909155

Printed and bound in Germany by Appl Druck Wemding

Set in Trade Gothic
Designed and typeset by Smith & Gilmour, London
Illustrations by Jason Lievesley

# CONTENTS

# FOREWORD

# FOREWORD
## BY EVAN DAVIS, BBC ECONOMICS EDITOR

I'm not a fan of books with titles like *Your Ideas Can Make You Rich*. You see them on airport book stands, raising false hopes and often glossing over the formidable challenges that arise in launching a new company.

At the very least, I always feel that in the interests of completeness, books such as this should have a subtitle that says *Your Ideas Can Also Make You Very Poor*. Even more so given that this is a *Dragons' Den* title, as, if you have a bad idea, the Dragons will spare you no humiliation in telling you how it will lose you money.

And perhaps that is the single most useful lesson that the world can draw from *Dragons' Den*: it's easier to screw up than succeed in business. If there were an easy way of creating a valuable business, someone else would have discovered it already. To coin a phrase often used by (American) economists, 'There are no $500 bills lying on the sidewalk'.

However *Dragons' Den* does also show that successful entrepreneurship defies class, background and education. The popularity of the programme appears to reflect a cultural shift towards the whole idea of starting a business, not just as a way of making money, but also as a means to career satisfaction. The shift is one the authorities are keen to promote – they know the economic value of a vibrant start-up sector. It is striking that business organisations have greeted the programme with enthusiasm.

But if you are banking on your dreams making you rich, don't expect the process to be as simple as gathering up carelessly discarded $500 bills. Experience tells us there *is* money on the pavement – it's just more likely to be small change than high denomination notes. That fundamental principle should always be the starting point of business planning.

And it's certainly borne out by the experiences in *Dragons' Den*. A good rule of thumb is that about 90 per cent of people who confront the Dragons go away with nothing. (The odds sometimes look better than that on television, because the producers

understandably include all the successful pitches while the failures are more likely to be edited out).

Looking at those who do leave empty-handed, I would put them into three similarly-sized categories.

Probably a third of them are simply never going to make a viable business. Notwithstanding the enthusiasm of the entrepreneurs, the dedication and the sweat they have invested in their idea, the best thing would be for them to ignore the usual encouragement that 'you should never give up'. They should give up, and the sooner the better.

When the Dragons point out their flaws in their uncompromisingly direct and honest style, it's not just good television; it's good advice.

There is a second group of would-be entrepreneurs who fail to attract an investment: those who have an idea that might actually make a viable business. Unfortunately, they do not seem to have the acumen or resources to see it through. Their idea is better pursued by someone else.

The final third are those who have a very good chance of creating a viable business, albeit not a very valuable one. They have a business that will sustain a lifestyle, rather than reap big rewards.

By and large the Dragons have not shown themselves too keen on investing in these businesses, even when they admire the work of the entrepreneur. Usually, they conclude that even if the business succeeds, it will not achieve a sufficient scale to make a big profit for an investor. Given that the Dragons have to ration their time and money, it's clear these businesses are not for them.

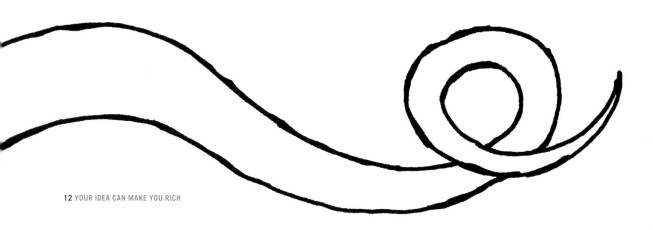

So much for the losers in *Dragons' Den*. Even looking at the 'winners', however, success is not assured. (I put winners in inverted commas as no one wins prizes in the show, rather they attract investments, for which they have to give away equity in their business). What you see on *Dragons' Den* is the beginning of the work, rather than the end.

If all this sounds a bit negative, it is meant to be. *Dragons' Den* often tells you more about what you should not do, than what you should. One of the miracles of the programme is that it usually avoids becoming unrelentingly dispiriting by offering enough opportunity, optimism and success to inspire its viewers.

But how can entrepreneurs entering the Den ensure they contribute to the positive side of the formula, rather than the negative? What makes for a successful encounter in *Dragons' Den?* It's hard to answer this question, as the Dragons themselves are not a uniform 'panel of experts'. They are a group of individuals, investing their own money, acting for themselves and not as a team. They often disagree with each other, which tells you that many judgements about business success are uncertain and subjective.

The Dragons also take very different approaches to analysing the opportunities in front of them. Doug Richard is probably the most scientific; he tends to focus on evidence that there is a market demand for the product involved. He hones in on the numbers in the business plan, and uses rules of thumb to value the opportunity in front of him.

Others, like Duncan Bannatyne, often appear more intuitive in their assessment of what will work and what will not, what will sell and what will not. They look at the numbers and do some maths, of course, but it never appears to be at the core of their decision.

Peter Jones is harder to categorise than the others. He is more eclectic. In some ways, he is more focussed on the character of the entrepreneur pitching to him, than the others are. When Peter invests, it sometimes seems to be an investment in the person in front of him, as much as in their business plan. And he certainly rejects people he dislikes. (Indeed, he is occasionally even fastidious about how the entrepreneurs dress when they stand before him).

Given this multiplicity of approaches, it's impossible to give a single formula for impressing them (or other investors). The Dragons have never drawn up a common list of criteria for success. If you were hoping to find their checklist here, you will be disappointed. If the Dragons had been asked to write this book, you would have had to wait several years for them to agree one text.

But their different approaches give an important clue as to the necessary attributes of successful entrepreneurs: they generally have to tick more than one box. They usually have to score well in the numbers and analysis side of things, and they have to score well on the human side as well.

Or, to put it another way, it is not sufficient to be impressive on the numbers side; it is not sufficient to give an engaging pitch; nor is it sufficient to have a good product around which you want to build a business. A true entrepreneur is likely to have all these attributes.

And that tells you as much about business as about *Dragons' Den*. You have to prepare on several fronts.

The first and most obvious thing is to have a decent business plan, one that demonstrates realistic projections of revenues, costs and profits.

A huge number of people have faltered in front of the Dragons; from having no business plan at all, or no memory of what's in it, or from having made untested and unreasonable claims about potential revenues and profits. They inevitably look like naughty school children brought before the Head for not doing their homework.

Some of them think they have hard evidence of a demand for their product, because friends, family and one or two associates have given it glowing reviews. The Dragons prefer to see evidence that someone who is *not* a friend or relative has actually forked out some real money for it, rather than politely said how much they like it.

Sometimes people come forward with a product that is already on the market, which is not selling well. If only they can get an investment, they say, marketing and sales will follow. The Dragons might be persuaded that sales can be turned around, but they will need to know why.

The hard analysis derived from spreadsheets and business plans helps enormously. It shows the business can be profitable, while projecting the facts and figures in an internally consistent way – from sales, cash flows, production capacity and costs, to office accommodation and staffing levels.

But as I have already said, getting the numbers right is not enough. Businesses are not made by computer. Successful entrepreneurs need more than good spreadsheet skills. They need some flair, some marketing acumen, some management skills, some imagination, and an ability to see opportunity.

Very often, when talking to the Dragons after an unsuccessful pitch, I hear one of them say words to the effect of: 'There was a good business in there somewhere, but that person has failed to see it'. It's a sad way for the core of a good idea to be lost.

On other occasions, when an investment *has* occurred in the show, the investing Dragon explains that although the business model was a bit flawed, the entrepreneur has all the skills necessary to get it right with only a little help.

Combining a well researched and elegantly constructed business plan, with insightful and shrewd business awareness is the best way to creating a successful business.

Alas, no book can deliver guaranteed business success; books can give some pointers, helping you avoid some egregious errors, prompting you to ask some useful questions, and filling you in on some of the experiences of others. But none of them have $500 bills tucked inside.

And while books can tell you some of the rules of the business game, so many rules are meant to be broken in business that nothing can provide a substitute for solid business judgement.

However, before this foreword becomes unduly negative about the challenges facing budding entrepreneurs, remember the real reason that *Dragons' Den* is uplifting is that entrepreneurs, by their nature, tend to be people who focus on the positive.

It's important for them to deal with potential business calamities rather as a construction worker on a suspension bridge has to deal with heights: he knows the drop is there, he plans for it, but he doesn't let the fear of falling cloud his judgement.

Most of us could not work at the top of a suspension bridge; most of us couldn't make it as a successful entrepreneur. But let's be thankful for those that try.

*Evan Davis*

'There's a fine line between being an entrepreneur and a dreamer.'
Duncan Bannatyne

# Chapter One
# ENTREPRENEUR OR DREAMER?

What, exactly, is an entrepreneur? We see the word all over the place; the Government is keen to foster the notion of Britain as a nation of entrepreneurs and the media – as exemplified in the television series *Dragons' Den* – is captivated by the entrepreneurial spirit. And no wonder. The idea of throwing off those corporate chains and working for oneself – as well as doing something inspiring, something that really drives you – is immensely appealing. In fact, in Britain, the freedom to adopt one's own approach to work is the key factor for people who are thinking of starting their own business. And, of course, there is the not insignificant matter of money. Those entrepreneurs who make it big get to benefit from the financial rewards – their ideas make them rich, not their bosses.

No surprise, then, that the nation's entrepreneurial spirit is alive and well, as demonstrated by the huge popularity of *Dragons' Den*. Many viewers secretly envied the hopeful entrepreneurs who braved the panel of fiery Dragons; no matter how they ended up, they all proved to have bucketfuls of ideas, enthusiasm, and determination, qualities many of us wish we had more of. Well, here's a revelation. **There's no difference between those people and you.** Anyone can be an entrepreneur. You don't need fancy qualifications but you do need a certain mindset and the right attitude – all of which will become clearer as you read on.

So what does it actually *mean* to be an entrepreneur? The word itself comes from Old French, meaning 'to undertake'. The *Oxford English Dictionary* defines the word, in a political and economic sense, as, 'One who undertakes an enterprise; one who owns and manages a business; a person who takes the risk of profit and loss.' It also cites one of the earliest-known applications of the word: 'One who gets up entertainments'. Which makes you realise that being an entrepreneur was once regarded as rather fun. Fun with a winning streak: the word also used to mean 'champion'

Today's entrepreneur would be well-advised to take note of the word's three crucial components: 'undertake', 'enterprise' and 'risk'. But be careful of the last word. No successful entrepreneur – least of all the Dragons in their TV Den – ever takes needless risks. Rather, they are not risk-averse. They *do* things. And doing anything carries a certain amount of risk: you can plan what you are going to do over and over again, but once you start doing it you can't always control the result.

The difference between an entrepreneur and a dreamer is, basically, in the doing. To be a dreamer, all you have to do is dream. Anyone can do that. We all do that. Many people dream of creating a hugely successful business and making vast amounts of money, but for most of them, the dream is pure fantasy. Making it real is the hard – and scary – part. So if you want to succeed,

make sure your dreams have a basis in reality and a realistic goal. Build your castles in the air, but build foundations under them. That's what this book is about. It's about helping you and your business idea to stand up. It's about doing. Because one thing's for sure: if you do nothing, nothing happens.

What is special about this book is that it examines, through real-life examples, that fine line – and, sometimes, the yawning gap – between dreamers and entrepreneurs. It draws on the experiences and emotions of real people who had real business ideas, which they pitched to real investors – who either did, or didn't, invest real money. Furthermore, these investors have all trodden the entrepreneurial route themselves. They may be called Dragons in the TV series in which they appear (and they may well breathe fire on ideas which they think deserve to be incinerated) but in the business world they and their ilk are known as business

angels and mentors. They are people who have successfully demonstrated entrepreneurial flair and who are willing to help others – those who seem to possess the right ideas, and ingredients, for success. Their help, of course, comes at a price: in exchange for money and advice, they'll want a stake in your business. They are not stupid. The phrase 'For fools rush in where angels fear to tread' may have been coined three hundred years ago by a poet, but it still resonates around today's pragmatic business world. And the angel syndrome isn't confined to a TV series. Nor is it new. Business angels and mentors form part of a growing investment community in this country. In our fast-moving and constantly changing society, it is usually easier and quicker (there's less bureaucracy) to secure investment from business angels than it is from other sources. This route is, arguably, where the future lies.

# SO JUST WHO ARE THE DRAGONS?

### DOUG RICHARD
Californian by birth, Doug is founder and Chairman of Cambridge-based data services company Library House, and co-founder of the Cambridge Angels (supporters of high-quality technology start-ups). He set up his first software venture in the '80s, and went on to become President and CEO of US software company Micrografx. Doug has a BA in Psychology from the University of California, a Juris Doctor from the School of Law (UCLA) and an Executive Management Certificate from the UCLA Anderson School of Business.

### DUNCAN BANNATYNE
A poverty-stricken childhood steeled Duncan's drive to make his fortune from an early age. He began his entrepreneurial life by trading in cars, but it was with an ice cream van that he changed the course of his life – setting out to become the king of the '99'. He then switched to nursing homes, becoming a multi-millionaire in the process. Since then, Duncan has built up a chain of health clubs called 'Bannatyne's'. Estimated to be worth around £130 million, Duncan has recently been awarded an OBE for services to business and charity. He was also North Region Entrepreneur of the Year 2003 and Master Entrepreneur of the Year 2003 for the North Region.

### PETER JONES
Peter joined the board of the electrical giants Siemens Nixdorf at the age of 28 – the youngest to do so. Peter's entrepreneurial journey started early, when at the age of 16, he founded a tennis academy. He then set up an IT accessories firm before joining Siemens Nixdorf, and then The Caudwell Group. Peter has since forged his own rival telecommunications firm, Phones International Group, which is now worth more than £300 million. Peter has won many national awards including Emerging Entrepreneur of the Year 2001, and is now considered to be one of the UK's leading businessmen.

### RACHEL ELNAUGH
Rachel was an accountant with Arthur Andersen when she got the idea for a business offering special gifts for special occasions. The resulting company, Red Letter Days, offers gift experiences such as driving grand prix cars or flying in jet aircraft. Red Letter Days is considered a model business for a new wave of British entrepreneurs and leads the market in gift experiences. Rachel's company now has an estimated worth of £25 million. Rachel is the only woman on the panel of Dragons.

Duncan Bannatyne

Peter Jones

## SIMON WOODROFFE

Armed with a desire to swap his well-established
career in the music business for piles of cash, Simon
Woodroffe has become the man behind restaurant
phenomenon Yo! Sushi. Simon cooked up the idea
for the space-age sushi bars with the help of a
Japanese acquaintance, who suggested 'a conveyor-
belt sushi bar with girls in PVC mini skirts'. Although
the PVC mini skirts never materialised, the Yo! brand
has grown considerably, and now boasts Yo! Japan,
Publishing Yo! and the forthcoming YOTEL! Simon
had a seat on the Dragon panel for the first series,
and his place is now occupied by:

Rachel Elnaugh

## THEO PAPHITIS

Theo started his working life at the age of 16
as a 'tea-stirrer's assistant' at Lloyds of London.
Aged 23, he started his first company, Surrey & Kent
Associates, dealing in commercial mortgage sales.
He then started acquiring ailing companies from
the receiver, and demonstrated his knack of turning
them into profit. Retailing is now at the core of an
empire which encompasses Ryman and La Senza,
but which also extends to football (he bought
Millwall football club in 1997) and the media.

Simon Woodroffe

Doug Richard

Some budding entrepreneurs profiled here and in the TV series remained firmly – for a variety of reasons – on the 'dreamer' side. Others wavered on the line, perhaps possessed of a good idea but with no means to see it through, no market research and no clear idea of who was going to benefit. In other words, a complete lack of business acumen. And some – the few who possessed all the right ingredients – crossed the line. There are lessons to be learned from all of them. The lessons from those who failed to secure investment from the Dragons are as interesting – perhaps even more so – than the lessons from those who succeeded.

For there seems to be another common denominator amongst successful entrepreneurs – THEY ARE NOT AFRAID OF FAILURE. Basic psychology would suggest that if you're terrified of failing then you either won't try or your fear will become a self-fulfilling prophecy and you will indeed fail.

**'Failure is the condiment that gives success its flavour.' Truman Capote**

## FAILURE

'I've never met anyone who went out to follow their dreams, who did what they wanted to do, and ended up regretting it – regardless of whether they succeeded or failed. But I've met many people who've said, "I wish I'd taken that chance when I had it".' – Simon Woodroffe

There's only one failure that really hurts: the failure to do what you want to do or what you intended to do. Other failures are never as destructive. In fact – and in business – they're often highly constructive. We learn more from our mistakes than we do from our successes. Look at it this way: if you get the wrong answer in a quiz, you want to know what the right answer is, don't you? You don't just want the information that 'you're wrong'. But if you get the right answer, you're unlikely to be interested in where you may have gone wrong if you'd chosen differently. On a broader level, it tends to be the *fear* of failure that overwhelms people, not the failure itself. Turn failure itself round; look at it differently. If you believe you can ski then you will persist in failing to ski until you can, actually, ski. But if you believe you can't ski, then you're right.

The point is to learn – to keep failing – until you achieve your goals. At least two unsuccessful visitors to *Dragons' Den* have done that. They failed to get what they wanted from the Dragons so they went elsewhere and succeeded in securing investment for their business ideas. They learned from their mistakes. Here's what Doug Richard said to one of them: 'Maybe this will be the best learning opportunity of your life and maybe you will go on to succeed.' The woman's 'failure' had been to demonstrate an extremely shaky grasp of figures and an apparent inability to tell the difference between gross profit and net profit. You can bet she didn't repeat that mistake. Duncan Bannatyne advised her that she should have had the relevant figures in her head and added, 'I think you'll probably regret not having done that today.' He said it kindly as well. Both Dragons were offering constructive criticism; an opportunity to learn.

'Perseverance is failing nineteen times and succeeding the twentieth.' – Julie Andrews (who climbed every mountain . . . )

'Experience is the name everyone gives to their mistakes.' – Oscar Wilde

'I have not failed. I've just found 10,000 ways that won't work.' – Thomas Edison

## SO, WHAT ARE THE INGREDIENTS FOR BECOMING A SUCCESSFUL ENTREPRENEUR?

There is no foolproof recipe for success as an entrepreneur. There are, however, some essential ingredients. (The cookery analogy is deliberate: there are umpteen books with recipes for lasagne, but they are all aiming to create the same basic end product. Lasagne.) So here are the core ingredients for entrepreneurs:

- Do it for passion, not money. If making money is your single motivating factor then you should probably try something different. Setting up in business may take far longer than you think and you may make very little money at first 'If I had to name a driving force in my life, I'd name passion every time.' – Anita Roddick, founder of The Body Shop

- Do something you know about. Philip Green, the retail mogul, has said that he only invests in retail businesses. That's what he knows about

- Have a clear mission or vision

- Be persistent 'If at first you don't succeed, try, try and try again. Then quit. No use in being a damn fool about it.' – W. C. Fields

- Don't be afraid to make mistakes. Mistakes are what we learn from

- Be self-disciplined

- Start getting good with money. Money is going to manage your business whether you like it or not

- Get yourself a mentor. Many of the successful pitchers that emerged from *Dragons' Den* did so, not just with money, but with the promise of sound advice. You can't work in a vacuum. You need advice, back-up and a sounding board. You need an unbiased person to tell you when you're going wrong

- Have a strong desire to succeed, both personally and financially

- Make sure that you work with people you like – and who like you 'The most important thing for me in business is to work with people I like. I don't like you.' – Rachel Elnaugh to a budding entrepreneur

- Be good to yourself. You don't want to burn out

- Make sure you are able to work as part of a team

- Be realistic 'I personally think the product is only deliverable in Disneyland because I think you live in Dreamland' – Peter Jones to a budding entrepreneur

- Make use of one of your most valuable assets – your common sense

## START-UP SECRETS
Ten out of ten entrepreneurs agreed that these
are the key ingredients for a successful start-up:

- An innovative idea

- The right market opportunity

- Selling ability

- An experienced team of people

- Contacts, both for business reasons and
  to gain advice

- Money: a realistic finance strategy is vital

- Time – lots of it

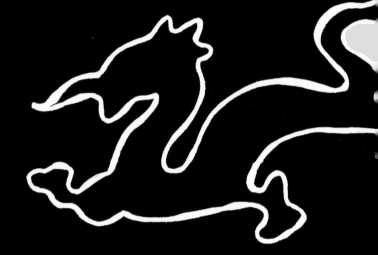

But, before any of this, you have to have IDEAS. You have to
be able to THINK CREATIVELY. Even those people who were
dismissed out of hand by the Dragons as having completely
unworkable ideas had . . . well, IDEAS. And they possessed the
courage to pursue them. The courage, in fact, to stand up in
front of a panel of five millionaire investors (plus a TV audience
of three million) and pitch. That takes guts. So add guts to the list.

# 'I did it my way.' Frank Sinatra

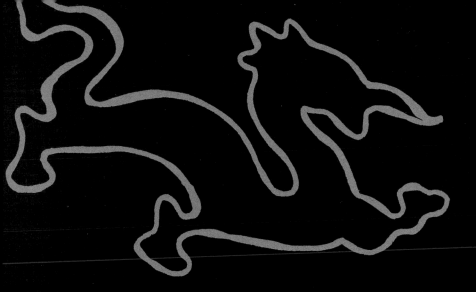

'Continuous effort –
not strength or
intelligence – is
the key to unlocking
our potential.'
**Winston Churchill**

# CREATIVE THINKING

## 'Imagination is more important than knowledge.' Albert Einstein

It just isn't true that some people have ideas and others don't. It is true, however, that some of us have lost – or, more accurately, mislaid – the ability to think creatively. All children possess that ability. Sadly, it's often diluted on the road to adulthood and discouraged through education. Ultimately, we arrive at a crossroads where 'Work' takes us in one direction and 'Play' the other. We take the former route because adults aren't really supposed to play. But why on earth not?

'We spend most of our lives working, so why do so few people have a good time doing it?' – Richard Branson

Instead we're allotted a short time for 'leisure' which, all too often, means dulling our brains with mindless entertainment. Entertainment doesn't have to be mindless. Remember that earlier definition of entrepreneur – 'one who gets up entertainments'? Think about it . . .

### TIPS FOR CREATIVE THINKING

Be open-minded, interested and involved. Get used to doing lots of things. Be with people. Ask questions. Listen. Receive. Ideas are not born in a vacuum – they spring from doing lots of different things. Being businesslike and being creative are often thought of as opposites. They're not.

Think of ideas as money; of money as ideas. Envisage your intellectual capital as a combination of skills, not as a static entity.

Think of the alignment of the right side of your brain – the 'creative' part – with the left side – the 'analytical' part. Left-brain hemispheres are associated with the intellect; right-brain hemispheres with intuition. Use your intuition. Potential investors in your business most certainly will. If the day comes for seeking investment, even though intellectually and on paper you may have the best idea and the best business plan, those investors may well turn you down because – and they'll probably couch this in different terms – 'something feels not quite right'. That 'something' is their intuition. It's invaluable.

Don't dismiss the stuff about brain hemispheres as a pseudo-scientific fad. It's the basis of much of today's research into cognitive neuroscience.

Ideas spring from all over the place. Successful *Dragons'*
*Den* entrepreneur Tracie Herrtage came up with her idea for
an innovative sofa when she was making cushions for her kids.
Another successful entrant had his brainwave for an umbrella-
vending machine when he came out of a tube station to find
it pouring with rain. The important thing is to get your ideas
into focus. Don't let them disappear into the realm of fantasy.
If you're thinking up an idea for a new business or a product,
try this approach. First of all, define clearly what your idea is.
Then ask yourself the following questions:

- What does it do?
- How does it benefit other people?
- Can the benefit be easily summarised in one sentence?
- Would you buy it yourself or recommend it to others?

Play with the idea a bit. Don't immediately start thinking along
the lines of 'If it's that simple it must already exist' and don't
think about the competition at this stage. That will kill the idea.
Give yourself time to play with it a bit longer.

Your idea may, in fact, already exist. Thomas Edison (he of the
light bulb) said, 'My principal business is giving commercial value
to the brilliant – but misdirected – ideas of others.' The stealing
of ideas is a fact of life, and, whilst you can take certain steps to
protect ideas (see Chapter Three), you can be sure that if you have
a viable proposition that you decide not to run with, then someone
else will. On the other hand, if you see your idea brought to life by
another company, don't immediately assume you've been ripped
off and start court proceedings. It is a fact of life that ideas have
a habit of appearing in the universe, to different people, at around
the same time. It's part of the phenomenon called synchronicity.

In your creative quest, you may come up with lots of sound and
original ideas. The problem is that few sound ideas are original,
and few original ideas are sound. It's those elusive few that
you're looking for.

# THE AGE OF INVENTION

Is there an optimum age to be an entrepreneur? Surprisingly, a recent study of 55,000 men and women who had patented inventions indicates that there is: 29 appears to be the perfect age to produce that flash of inspiration, to develop and go with that breakthrough idea. The report of a US study – *The Burden of Knowledge and the Death of Renaissance Man: Is Innovation Getting Harder?* – suggests that the ideal combination of education and energy comes at the end of our third decade. It was then, for example, that Alexander Graham Bell submitted his patent for the telephone, one of the greatest inventions of modern times. Quentin Tarantino was 29 when he wrote and directed Reservoir Dogs. And Stelios Haji-Ioannou was in his twenty-ninth year when he revolutionised air-travel by founding easyJet. A century ago, the age of peak performance was even younger, usually the early twenties. Over the last hundred years, innovators have, apparently, become progressively older.

So are you over the hill if you're over 30? Well, no. The same report concludes that innovation is now harder than it used to be because the burden of knowledge is greater. Leonardo da Vinci, arguably the greatest creative genius the world has ever seen, not only painted masterpieces but designed prototypes for, amongst other devices, tanks, submarines and aeroplanes. But he had, so the theory goes, more innovative space to play with, because he had fewer other innovations to contend with.

On the other hand, da Vinci remained innovative well into his old age. Lots more 'stuff' had been invented by then (often by him), yet he kept on generating ideas. So that flies in the face of the ageist theory of innovation. And of the 'burden of knowledge' theory.

Da Vinci died in 1519. With the huge amount of knowledge we've acquired in the last five hundred years, there should be no need, indeed no point, in inventing anything more – yet we still go on inventing. Charles Duell, of the US Office of Patents, thought we'd reached saturation point over a century ago. In 1895, he said that 'Everything that can be invented has been invented.' Clearly, he hadn't watched *Dragons' Den* . . .

Incidentally, 1895 appears to have been a really bad year for foresight. In Britain that year, Lord Kelvin, President of the Royal Society, declared that 'heavier-than-air flying machines are impossible' . . .

The serious point here is actually extremely serious: it just isn't possible to apply logic to the idea that there's now less room for innovation. It's like trying to prove – or disprove – something that doesn't yet exist.

## THE THEORY OF INCOMPLETENESS

Which brings us to Kurt Godel, the famous Czech-born mathematician. In 1931 (he was 37, by the way) he demonstrated his Theorem of Incompleteness, one of the most important theories of modern times. Applying it initially to mathematics, he proved that by using rules and axioms, there will always be propositions that cannot be proved either true or false. The problem is that those rules and axioms themselves are limited by their own set of rules.

Godel's theorem has been extrapolated into the wider world and has been used to argue, for example, that a computer can never be as clever as a human being because the extent of a computer's logic is limited by its own fixed set of axioms. The theorem has also been applied to some scientific breakthroughs: they're not actually 'breakthroughs' – they're discoveries that cannot be explained by the set of rules and axioms we've previously used to explain science. So they require us to draw up a new set of rules that will explain them – until we discover something else that appears inexplicable and we devise a new set of rules to explain *them* . . .

You can apply this to business. Go and look at old books of 'rules' about how to succeed in business or make a fortune out of your idea. They keep changing. And that's because people keep doing things – and succeeding with them – that don't fit into the rules. Godel's Theorem breaks all the rules. It implies that you'll never really understand yourself (or anybody else) because the human mind can only be sure of what it knows about itself by relying on what it knows about itself.

So where does this leave you as an entrepreneur? It should tell you that whether you are 12 or 92, **nobody actually knows whether or not your innovation or business idea will work**. Sure, they can give their opinions and their – often extremely valuable – advice and expertise. But they will be basing much of that advice on rules and axioms. If your idea is a winner, the rules will have to change. They always do.

Look at one of the most successful businesses of modern times – the movie business. There are countless people paid vast sums to ensure that their company's next film will be a real money-spinner. There are also innumerable books on how to write a best-selling script and make millions out of it. Yet one of the best-known things about Hollywood is the phrase coined by William Goldman, possibly the film world's most eminent screenwriter and chronicler of the movie business. He distilled the essence of Hollywood into just three words: 'Nobody Knows Anything'. Even more interesting, nobody in Hollywood has ever bothered contradicting him . . .

# 'If the world should blow itself up, the last audible voice would be that of an expert saying, "It can't be done".' Peter Ustinov

Yet it's always worth listening to sound advice. And as regards your age and experience, there are a few pointers that emerged from the *Dragons' Den* that would serve you well. You don't, obviously, have to be young to be an entrepreneur – but by the same token, youth and inexperience can work to your advantage. If, for example, you've just left university you will be used to financial insecurity, to irregular hours and, possibly, to staying up half the night. (You'll be doing that a lot if you're an entrepreneur, although for rather different reasons.)

But emerging from permanent employment to pursue your dreams is no barrier to becoming a successful entrepreneur. It could even provide the fuel to fire your ambition. This is something your job may not have done. Statistics indicate that it may, in fact, have all but killed your ambition. According to a study by the Conference Board, a US business research organisation, only half of Americans are satisfied with their jobs. A quarter said they were 'simply showing up to collect the pay check'. And those earning more than $50,000 a year were only slightly happier than those earning less than $15,000. Not good, is it?

So quitting your job may well be the best thing you've ever done. But if you're looking for funding for your new venture, you've got to be quite clear about whether or not you are going to quit. Going part-time is having your cake and eating it. It may imply a lack of commitment to any potential investor in your business. And whether they're Dragons or angels, if they perceive a lack of commitment, they're going to breathe fire on your idea. In fact, that's exactly what they did.

The inventors of a golfing product, in which Peter Jones was extremely interested, fell at two hurdles – the most significant being the unwillingness of one of them to leave his job with a recruitment company. The product was already in production and selling: it needed a greater degree of commitment behind it. If the inventors were unwilling to demonstrate that commitment, why should anyone else?

Similarly, a man who had pioneered an all-year-round plant watering system almost sold the idea to the Dragons – until he declared that he couldn't give a full-time commitment as he was working on a research dissertation. The Dragons immediately lost interest. Later it transpired that he had been a little disingenuous about his negotiating position in the first place.

Yet over-commitment can be off-putting as well. In fact, as Simon Woodroffe says, 'Possibly the most off-putting aspect of a pitch is when someone is convinced beyond reason that their product will work.' One such example was the inventor of a mat that was supposed to absorb the odours of dogs, as well as those of smelly shoes. The Dragons heaped scorn on the entire concept but were especially aghast to hear that, having done absolutely no test marketing of the mat, the inventor was, as Rachel Elnaugh put it, 'prepared to give up a job in IT for the sake of an odour eater'.

The problem with the above examples – although in some cases the problem was only one of many – appears to be a lack of clarity when it comes to personal goals.

# PERSONAL GOALS

You could do a lot worse than begin your entrepreneurial career by writing a personal development plan. It's surprising how many people don't actually define what they want out of life, let alone their business. If you haven't set your own personal goals then you're unlikely to be able to focus on what your product or business can do for others.

What exactly are your areas of excellence? What are your desires and needs? To what extent are you prepared to stretch your income, relationships, your time and your health to achieve them? Why are you the best person to develop your idea? What does success mean to you? Why do you want to be successful? What's the level of income that you see yourself happy with? In answer to the last question, if you don't know, don't care or are prepared to starve to achieve a level of success then you're either a truly exceptional person or you're totally unrealistic. Especially about money.

# MONEY – THE BOTTOM LINE

This book costs money. The reason you bought it or were given it is because you want to make money. And if you stole it then that's about money as well – you didn't want to part with any. In the end, it's always about money.

But what about in the beginning? *Your Idea Can Make You Rich*. Did you begin to read this book because you have an idea, or purely because you like the idea of being rich? Yes, your idea can make you rich, but only if your passion for the idea is greater than your passion for wealth. Look at the panel of Dragons. Like most other entrepreneurs, they were, first and foremost, passionate about their ideas. Getting rich was the bonus. Money was not the primary motivator.

So before you start planning exactly how you're going to make your idea work, you need to be aware of what you *really* think about money. Do you respect it? Do you spend it, save it or does it seem to slip through your fingers? What do you think more money will do for you?

In our consumer culture, money equals an emotional hit. We're trained to equate the right car/clothes (i.e. the spending of money) with happiness and the right partner. We tend *not* to be trained to respect money and to balance it properly.

So, for most people 'enough' money is seldom enough. Research into lottery winners has shown that, sooner or later – usually sooner – most winners of vast amounts of money return to the same state of emotional happiness that they started from. The same goes for people who worked for their money: 'Of all the billionaires I have known, money just brings out the basic traits in them. If they were jerks before they had money, they are simply jerks with a billion dollars.' – Warren Buffett

Money and the material goods it provides does not fundamentally change people. It doesn't make them happier and don't assume it's going to make you happier either. In fact, despite increased longevity, better health and unprecedented prosperity, most people in the developed world are no happier than they were fifty years ago. It would, of course, be ludicrous to say that money is not important. At the very least, as Woody Allen said, 'Money is better than poverty, if only for financial reasons.'

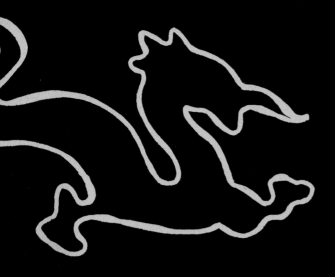

'The man with a new idea is a crank, until the idea succeeds.'
Mark Twain

Yet the above does serve to underline the fact that, as a primary motivator, money has little to do with success. If anything, it obscures the need to set yourself goals. So be cautious before equating success with money. Be cautious, in fact, about the concept of success. Bob Dylan had a good definition: 'A man is a success if he gets up in the morning and goes to bed at night and in between does what he wants to do.'

## 'Success is the ability to go from failure to failure without losing your enthusiasm.' Winston Churchill

And as regards it bringing happiness: 'The secret of a happy life is to do work you enjoy and then you'll be too busy to know whether you're happy or not.' – George Bernard Shaw

So if you're reading this purely because you want to make a quick buck then go and read something else. Your motives are dodgy. You are outnumbered because, in Britain, **the greatest single motivator for considering starting a business is the freedom to adopt one's own approach to work.**

Yet money *is* going to pass through your fingers on your entrepreneurial journey. Possibly quite a lot of it. And attitudes to money are surprisingly complex. Try asking yourself a few questions about it:

- Do you know how much money you keep in your bank account?
- Do you account for your money? If not, why not?
- Do you take note of where your money goes? Of how much you spend on yourself?

Try it for a while. Down to the last cup of coffee. It's called a balance sheet.

# 'Work is more fun than fun.' Noël Coward

If you're going to be a successful entrepreneur you're going to need to know all about balance sheets. If you monitor your own expenses for a week you may reach some surprising conclusions. You may discover that you are not spending according to your true needs but frittering your money away. For example, you might think a visit to the theatre is too expensive but spend the equivalent of a decent ticket on cups of coffee most weeks. What may emerge is that, like many people, you have a totally erratic relationship with money. You may find that you don't actually respect it. And if you don't respect your own money, why are you going to respect someone else's?

There's a Russian proverb: 'There are two fools in every market. One asks too little, one asks too much.' One of the most commonly recurring themes of entrepreneurs who entered *Dragons' Den* was precisely this. People were very unfocused about how much money they were going to need to pursue their ventures. Some asked for too little, others asked for too much. Sure, other variables – some of them unknown – come into play in a business environment, but the essential thing is to be aware of your own attitude to money. The buck stops with you, and if you haven't got a clear idea of where your own money goes, then you're unlikely to be able to monitor anyone else's.

And if you can balance your own books you're well on the way to finding the correct balance between money and success. Neither of them is about fast cars and large yachts (remember that fantasy stuff). Both are far more complex and creative than that. Fundamentally, they're about self-knowledge, about peace of mind and the notion that you know yourself and know what you want. They are also about good health and an abundant attitude. If you're emotionally overdrawn or a binge spender you're not in the best position to be a successful entrepreneur. But if you have a sense of well being and get enough sleep, enough exercise, and enough food and love, then you're well on the way. The rest is down to you, your idea, your motivation – and of course, your marketing…

# FROM THE DRAGON'S MOUTH: DOUG RICHARD

Doug Richard has extensive experience as both entrepreneur and angel. A former senior executive of both public and private technology companies in the US and Europe, he is the founder and Chairman of Library House.

'Starting a business is not a mystery and it's not magic. That's partly why I'm doing *Dragons' Den*; to help showcase entrepreneurship, to help drive the mystery out of starting a business, to show that that it's do-able.

*Dragons' Den* is a snapshot of the early stages of investment. There is no doubt that the businesses we see are far too early for institutional investment, and far too risky for banks. They've usually already been to what we've referred to on the show as "friends, family and fools". The next stage is angel investment. In this case, the *Dragons' Den*.

The only magic involved is the magic of television. The BBC does a good job of capturing the story being told, but what you don't see is that, if one of the Dragons shows interest, the story can go on for hours. Even so, we are operating under the constraints of investing in an uncommonly short period of time! In the normal course of events it usually takes me four months to make an investment, so however long I spend in that one interview in the *Dragons' Den*, it's still considerably shorter. I think it's important to communicate that in the real world you'll have many meetings with an interested investor. This is different.

What *isn't* different – and this is where I think the show delivers a very valuable point – is that if you do not capture the interest of the investors in a reasonably short period of time then your first meeting will be your last. *Dragons' Den* highlights – accurately – that if you cannot make a concise and cogent case for your business then no investor is going to invest.

That's where I see one of the differences between the first and the second series. It's absolutely clear to me that entrepreneurs had seen the first series and had prepared themselves in an effort to respond to what they thought were the issues that concerned us. My first concern, my fundamental preoccupation, is, "Have they thought first and foremost about the customer?" The people who get it right are those who can clearly articulate the product or service and its benefit to the customer. People are now much better at getting the core numbers, at not treating them as ceremonial things that an accountant does. That's a bad thing to do – the numbers *are* the business. And the successful people also now describe more accurately which stage of the business they are at, how they're going to use the funds, and how their business will be aided by an angel investor rather than another type of investor. They are also the ones who stand up to hard questioning without being rude; the ones who stand their ground, answer questions and keep it dispassionate.

I would say, from the first series, that *Grails* (the bespoke clothing company) was an almost perfect case study. I invested in the founder, Tracey Graily, more than the business. She had a lot of attributes I look for. She had extensive prior business experience and a passion for product and service. She was very resilient in facing questions. And she was able to describe very precisely what the customer wanted and how she was going to achieve it. In terms of core deliverables, she got it right.

To me, the act of starting a business requires planning and preparation of a very specific, structured type. When I think about investing I use exactly the same structured questions and answers as I would use if I were starting the business myself. There are four areas I look at, and I look at them in order. Firstly, the benefit. This covers both the product and the service. What is the benefit? Who is the customer? What are the attributes that define the customer by type? What kind of product is it? Will it change the way people operate, the way businesses behave, or will it simply be faster or cheaper?

The second question is about the people involved. For me, the number one critical question is, "Can this person afford to do this? Are they in a position to go without much money and can they give up their time?" The other big people question is, "Do they have other people with them to make up a successful team or, if not, do they understand what they're going to need?"

Thirdly, I address the market. How big is it? How accessible? What about competitors and distributors? People go wrong in some respects here – you always do – but I'm looking for evidence that people have thought this out in an informed and structured way.

The fourth question is the investment case. What is the potential for return and how long will it take? If I can't make money then this is *not* a good thing . . .

Business qualifications? I don't think an MBA, for example, is either a good or a bad thing in the entrepreneurial context – but I do think they are essentially only useful when they are informed by real business experience. I didn't bother going back to get any real business education until I'd had business experience. It was incredibly valuable because I could relate it back to the business I was in and tie it to the things I understood. But you don't need business qualifications to deliver a cogent case about how a product can deliver something to someone. Again, I'm looking, first and foremost, for people who have thought about the customer and the benefit.'

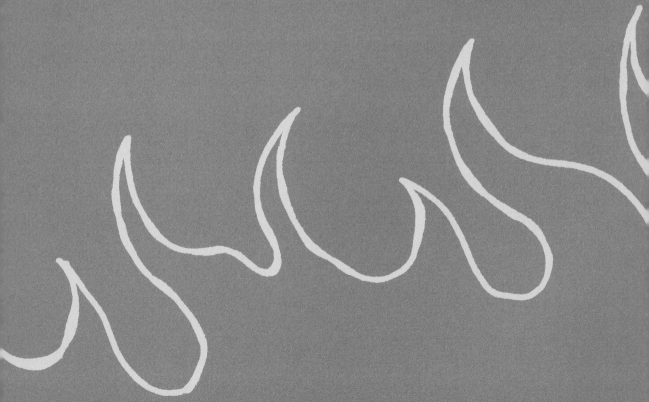

'Money flows from giving people what they want.' **Rachel Elnaugh**

# Chapter Two
# YOUR MARKET

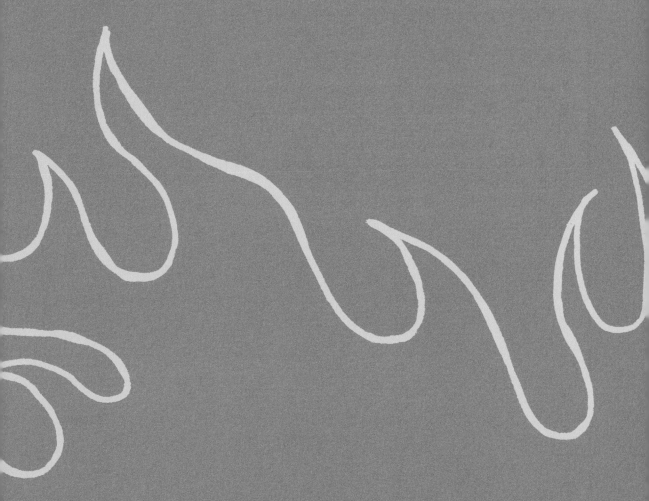

So you have come up with a stunningly brilliant idea. (You have, you have.) But what do you do with it? What are the first steps you take to see if it's a viable business proposition? If you're going to bask in your brilliance you have to do more than just be an innovator. You can't build a reputation on what you're going to do with your idea; your reputation can only come from other people. And the people who will make or break your reputation live in a place called the market. The marketplace.

Here's a simple definition of the market: buyer + seller = transaction = market. The crucial ingredient is the presence of the seller. You would be amazed how many people just make the assumption that their product will sell without bothering to go anywhere near the market themselves. Here's a simple definition of the word assumption: 'presumption; arrogance'. Arrogance gets a good seeing-to later in this book. And it's safe to say that, in business, no one should ever assume anything.

The good news is that you don't have to have a marketing background to get to grips with basic marketing. If you have a hefty dose of common sense, it may well actually be an advantage *not* to have a background in marketing or business strategy. Marketing and market research are vital disciplines, but their basic ingredients can all too easily disappear under a deluge of buzzwords. You don't need buzzwords or marketing gurus to help you. You just need to follow some fairly basic steps.

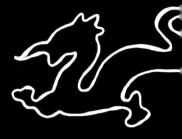

## YOUR BACKGROUND

A significant number of budding entrepreneurs seeking investment in the *Dragons' Den* said they had backgrounds in marketing. But what does this actually mean? 'Marketing' can be something of a catch-all phrase. The fact is, we can all claim to have experience in this field. One way or another, we're marketing ourselves all the time. It's also a fact that marketing skills are essential ingredients for the successful entrepreneur. But if you've got the right personality and the right idea and pitch it in the right way then, relevant background or not, you're innately good at marketing.

But you don't *need* to tick the 'marketing' box in answer to the questions about your background. You do, however, need to be prepared for questions about that background. Sure, it helps to have experience of the cut-and-thrust of the commercial world, but if you don't, then *be honest* about it. One of the reasons you're approaching others for help may be that you need business advice as much as you need investment. One unsuccessful entrant, seeking investment to turn a ruined Scottish castle into a time-share business, admitted that he had no experience in property development and had spent his working life as the 'lowest of the low' in the tourist industry. The Dragons were utterly charmed by him. True, they didn't give him any money, but it was actually his idea – more romantic than realistic – that failed to convince them. His background was . . . well, his background. You are what you are. Your lack of business background will not, on its own, preclude you from getting investment.

The Petty brothers, with their IVCam invention, illustrated this. They were, by their own admission, almost completely clueless about business – but they secured a pledge of investment from the Dragons. Again, they were straightforward about their backgrounds. They were engineers, not businessmen. Often in *Dragons' Den* it was actually people *with* backgrounds in marketing and advertising who antagonised the Dragons. The reason? They gilded the lily; they made sweeping claims that didn't quite stand up to close scrutiny. So don't claim – as one budding entrepreneur did – that you 'launched Sky TV'. You didn't. You know you didn't. You may have been involved with the launch but you are not Rupert Murdoch.

So the 'right' background doesn't count for much if you have the wrong attitude. Nor does it help if you're going to cling to your background at the expense of moving forward. One hopeful entrepreneur, and winner of numerous design awards, aroused the Dragons' interest – and then dampened it with the news that he couldn't commit full-time. Commitment, as discussed in Chapter One, is vital.

And what about a background in business education? Surely it helps if you can thrust your marketing module in the faces of potential investors? Actually, it doesn't. While it would be wrong to say that any form of education is a hindrance, it can, in the entrepreneurial environment, be a double-edged sword (see Chapter Three). And it certainly won't give you a VIP pass into the *Dragons' Den*. To date, only one of the entrepreneurs (the business partner of an inventor) who emerged from the Den with investment had a degree in business.

Ideally, your background should complement your bid to become an entrepreneur. But it doesn't have to control it – and it doesn't belong in the foreground. That place should be occupied by your customer. If you can describe, very precisely, what your product or service is, what your customer wants and how you are going to fulfil those desires, then you are on very solid ground.

# WHAT BUSINESS ARE YOU IN?

What sort of question is that? You've come up with a revolutionary new idea for a hotel, so you're in the hotel business. You already know the answer to that one. Move on . . .

. . . But hold on. You're in the hotel business. You're planning to go and ask someone for money for your new hotel. But what, exactly, *is* the business of your hotel? Unless your idea is revolutionary to the point of insanity, your hotel, like every other hotel, will have bedrooms. So, in effect, you're planning to go and ask someone for money so that you can build bedrooms. (It's beginning to sound rather unexciting, isn't it?)

You're going to have to rethink. And you're going to have to rethink **in terms of what sort of business or service you're providing to the customer**. Is your hotel providing great food? Or is fantastic accommodation the thing? Or, now that you're thinking about it, is it going to be best as a holiday venue? Who for? Honeymoon couples or families with children? Or is it actually, what with all the sporting facilities you're providing, a superb venue for an activity weekend break? What about hosting corporate events? On the other hand, maybe all those floaty spa and therapy ideas you had would make your hotel the best place in the world for a relaxing, holistic healing experience?

It all begins to look rather more complicated when you take a customer-based approach. It gets even more complex when you refine your thinking and investigate beyond providing specific products and services for customers – instead, focusing on **customer needs**.

Let's say you've decided that you will make your fortune by manufacturing a new and terrific range of pens. That's what you do. You make pens. Terrific pens. Simple. But, from the point of view of meeting customer needs, that isn't what you do at all. You're actually fulfilling the need to write. By looking at it from the customer-fulfilment angle, you're really getting to the nub of the matter. Who needs to write? Why do they write? What do they write? What do they normally write *with*? If they don't normally use pens, why are they going to start? What are the advantages of pens? What are the advantages of other pens? What, specifically, is the advantage of *your* type of pen?

Look at that last question again. Hopefully you will find that you now have two quite different answers to it. The first is the one that you had all along and is based on the wonderful and unique qualities of your pen. The second is based on customer needs and it's about fulfilling those needs. You want to pay very, very close attention to the second answer. It's the one that will get you to the marketplace.

## YOUR ASPIRATIONS

That's easy as well. You want to become rich as a result of your idea. That's probably why you bought this book. It said *Your Idea Can Make You Rich*. Well, yes it can, but as we already know, money doesn't work as a primary motivator. It doesn't wash as a business goal either. Nor does aspiring to become the greatest entrepreneur or even the market leader. Your aspirations should be firmly grounded in your business and, by implication, in the benefit you are bringing to your customers.

Tracey Graily, one of the investment winners in the *Dragons' Den*, made an interesting – and very emphatic – remark about her business aspirations. Although her company made bespoke clothes and provided advice and consultations for hard-working, cash-rich/time-poor women, the aspirations she cited had nothing to do with clothes. Her business, she said to the Dragons, was about **making life easier** for her target customers.

The picture that should be emerging is that by identifying precisely what business you are in, and by addressing your exact aspirations, you are also beginning to identify your target market. If you have correctly focused on what customers in your business need and have identified which of those needs you can fulfil, you're already zeroing in on a target. Now you want to hit that target.

## YOUR MISSION

Hit it with your mission-stick. This is a statement that will incorporate the mission that you had in Chapter One with the information that you now know. In an ideal world, a mission statement will announce, in one sentence, what benefit you're offering and why it's unique. This is the statement you can take to the world and communicate to everyone in your business environment. It's the foundation for a marketing plan or a strategy.

Here's Microsoft's mission statement. If it were just one sentence then maybe Microsoft would be ranked Number 1 in the FT Global 500. But it takes up three sentences. Maybe that's why they're ranked third. Still, a valuation of $262,974.9 million isn't bad for the brainchild of a couple of entrepreneurs, is it?

Microsoft exists, the company states, **'to help people and businesses throughout the world realise their full potential. This is our mission. Everything we do reflects this mission and the values that make it possible.'**

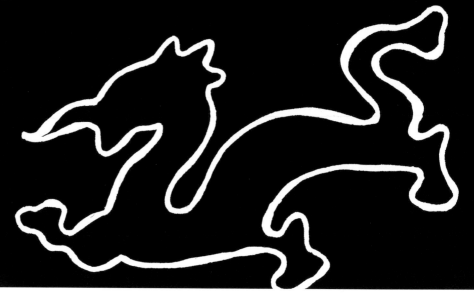

# MARKET RESEARCH

People often think they need in-depth analyses, industry-by-sector reports, breakdowns of trends and statistics, market segmentation, customer demographics and, well . . . lots of graphs and charts and whatnot in order to conduct market research. Yes, you'll be doing yourself a huge favour by doing as much research as possible. It's absolutely critical to starting a business and launching a product so the more you do, the better. But you can also take some simple initial steps to test the water.

Your first and easiest – yet, arguably, most essential – step should be to talk to people who are passionate about your area of innovation. If you think you've come up with a great gardening concept, then go and talk to people who are passionate about gardening. It's a truism across all areas of life **that people love talking about themselves and their passions**. Go and find them – and find a way to interest them. Get them involved. Ask their advice. Don't worry about divulging the revolutionary secrets of your idea; just inform them of the basic principles of it. (It's also a truism that when people are talking passionately about their areas of knowledge they often don't listen to you anyway. They're too busy talking. Absorb what they're saying.)

What people **don't** like is to be ambushed. A full-on approach is at best tactless and at worst extremely annoying. If you approach with all guns blazing then people will try to hide from you or they will tell you to get lost. This is not what you want. You want as much advice as you can get. (Not, by the way, advice from – to coin a phrase from the *Dragons' Den* – 'friends, family and fools'.)

What you're also doing is dipping your toes into the water. By talking to people who know about what you're trying to do, you'll get an idea of how your proposition sounds. Yes, they may think your idea sounds barking, but that's not the point at this stage. If, by articulating it, *you're the one* who thinks it sounds barking, then you've done yourself a favour. But if this, the first public airing of what you're planning, sounds viable, then you may well have found an opportunity. And an opportunity in business is, at its most basic, a scenario wherein you sell something to someone else and make a profit.

> **'A pessimist sees the difficulty in every opportunity. An optimist sees opportunity in every difficulty.'**
> **Winston Churchill**

Thomas Edison advised entrepreneurs and inventors 'to find out everything everybody else knows, and then begin where they left off'. Talking to people who have knowledge, then, is your first port of call in your investigations.

Once you've done this, if you still believe there's an opportunity in the offing, find out more. Find out things like:

- Where do your consumers come from? Are they tourists or townies, suburbanites or from the 'shires'?
- What's their age group?
- What are their buying patterns?
- What's the competition and how does it target the market?
- Who *influences* the competition? Can *you* influence *them*?

There's a wealth of information available about consumers and markets. Much of it is free and a lot of it is easily accessible. Trade associations, libraries, Business Link advisories and your local Chamber of Commerce are all good places to start.

In some cases, and depending on your business idea, the market research you'll need to undertake may be remarkably simple. But don't tell this to marketing professionals. They will get cross and tell you that you're wrong.

An example of this from the *Dragons' Den* was the research undertaken by Charles Ejogu, who successfully pitched for funding for his umbrella-vending machine. The idea was to initially place the product – a vending machine that not only sold umbrellas but also carried advertising – in London Underground stations. The steps, as outlined by Charles to the Dragons, were straightforward (do not confuse this word, by the way, with 'easy'). He found out if the idea had already been done, discovered that it hadn't, designed the machine, and then approached London

Underground to try to secure the exclusive rights across the entire network. It took him over a year, but he succeeded.

As regards the market, there are numerous statistics available about the people who use the London Underground as well as about the network itself. Figures relating to peak travel times; the busiest stations; the stations with the largest concourses and passenger demographics have all been published. Charles Ejogu *used* these statistics, and by doing so was able to target the stations that would be most suitable for his product. (There are also statistics available about the likelihood of rain falling in London. Suffice to say it's pretty likely . . . )

In sharp contrast to the above – as regards both product and market – was the pitch for an idea to launch, in the entrepreneur's own words, 'an annual, exclusive contemporary arts and music weekend event located in a central London park'. This initial premise sounded rather appealing. Unfortunately, the Dragons couldn't get beyond that premise ('What exactly happens at this event?' Doug Richard.) It didn't seem that the entrepreneur had got much beyond that either. Although he proposed that 'over 30,000 members of the public would be paying £35 per day to come together to enjoy an unforgettable evening' (armed, hopefully, with Charles Ejogu's umbrellas), it didn't become clear exactly who these people might be, nor what they were coming to see. The putative organiser anticipated that 75 per cent of them would be coming to listen to the live music but conceded that there was, in fact, no live music booked. And as regards the restaurant facilities, the 'very strong relationship with Pizza Express' turned out to be neither a sponsorship agreement nor a contract. The entrepreneur's own role didn't seem clearly defined either. 'I am,' he said, 'an entrepreneur. I work alongside people and produce projects.'

If you're trying to separate canny businesspeople from £100,000 of their money, this *really* isn't the way to do it. The point, however, isn't to make fun of people who failed in the *Dragons' Den*, but to see their failure as a learning curve. (In marketing terms, to 'reposition' that failure.)

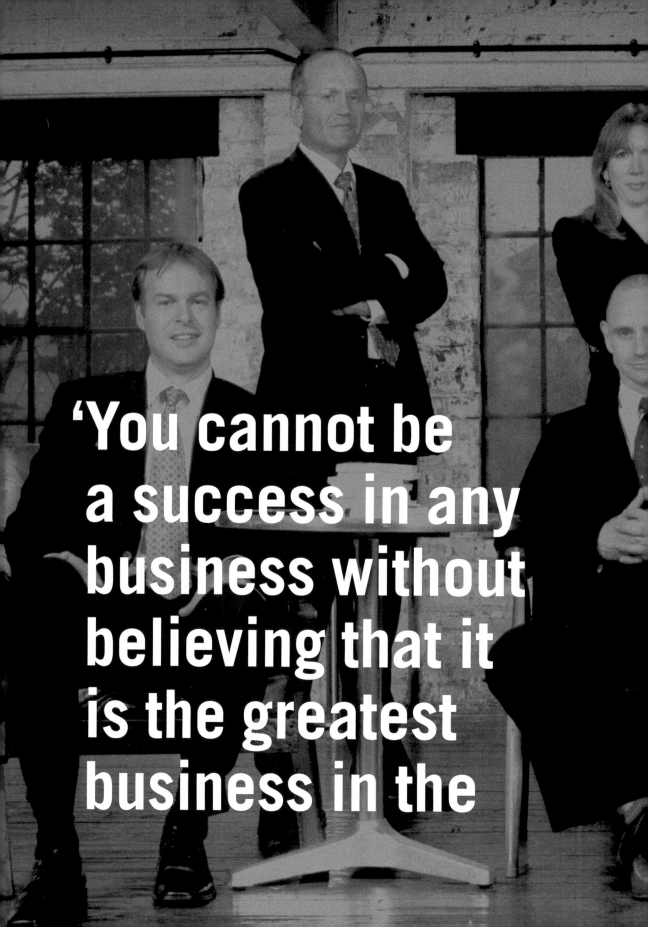

'You cannot be a success in any business without believing that it is the greatest business in the

world . . . You have
to put your heart
in the business
and the business
in your heart.'
Thomas Watson Snr

Success would have been more likely if the pitch
had addressed issues like:

- How many people go to outdoor art and music festivals in London
- How many such festivals currently exist
- Why people go to them. The music may well be only one reason
- It may not even be the main one
- Why your event will be different. This is crucial
- Why bands play at outdoor festivals
- Why *you* are the person to make it happen

## CHRISTENING YOUR IDEA

Names are important. They're vital. You'll want your name to become a brand. And you certainly don't want the naming process to be a baptism by fire. Or, indeed, laughter. One memorable *Dragons' Den* entrant had an idea for a chain of hair blow-drying salons. What was she going to call them? asked one of the Dragons. 'Blow,' she replied with a straight face. There were no straight faces at the other end of the room . . .

If you don't have any money (which, let's face it, is quite likely at this stage) you probably won't be about to carry out a survey through a market research company. You could, however, run your own focus group by showing your product, in conjunction with competing products, to any people you can persuade to attend your own group. Remember, people like being involved. You can also review industry trends by contacting the associations and organisations in the sector you are trying to penetrate. Large organisations regularly survey buying trends and highlight issues that concern the whole market. The Internet is a good place to start this research.

The Internet is also a place where you can develop that research. It's not a bad thing to try to create a sense of community around your product: to offer tips, opinion postings and surveys. Remember again that people like being involved. But do bear in mind that this sort of activity is largely for your own benefit. Unless your messing-about on the Internet can lead to proof of the viability of your product and, consequently, sales, potential investors won't be very interested in the number of 'hits' you get.

Offline, too, there are good opportunities for getting you and your product seen. You can join membership associations, help with community-based events, even get customers together. Thinking big but starting small are perfectly compatible. One could go as far as to say they're essential. Thinking big and starting big are unlikely bedfellows. And the combination is unlikely to appeal to investors. In the *Dragons' Den*, one entrant was intending to start five businesses at once. He was roundly told off for being too unrealistic; for wanting too much, too soon. If your idea is on this sort of scale, the chances are that it's all about you, the grandiosity of yourself and your fiscal ambitions – not about the customer.

## PROVING A CONCEPT

The best way to convince someone that your idea is worth investing in is to prove that it sells. And the only way to prove that it sells is to have people buy it. If you're seeking investment for an *idea* for a business, you cannot, obviously, do this. Instead, you have to use every set of variables based on your market and product research to convince investors of the likelihood of people buying your product.

For inventors, proving a concept can, in the first instance, often be fairly simple. You make your product and then you find people who will give you money for it. That's it. What you *don't* do is tell potential investors that your family and friends think your product is marvellous and that it will sell.

One entrepreneur in the *Dragons' Den* had a particularly bad time trying to secure investment for his odour-absorbing dog blanket. He had conducted product research and could claim with confidence that 'There's nothing like it in the UK, there's nothing like it in Europe and, as far as I'm aware, there's nothing like it in the rest of the world.'

Fine. But there was no evidence of *market* research. Was he aware of whether or not anybody actually *wanted* this mat?

Well, not really. His family and friends apparently thought it was a great idea – but people can think what they like. Duncan Bannatyne did: 'Your friends and family are wrong. You're wrong.'

Doug Richard went straight to the crux of the matter. 'I don't understand what problem you're solving. My dog loves her blanket. It smells. When it gets really rank it gets put in the washing machine. My dog also smells. My kids wash the dog. So we wash the dog and the blanket. What's the problem?'

The problem was the lack of proof of the concept. Doug Richard, it's true to say, was merely relating his own experiences. There may well be other families who wash neither their dog nor its blanket and who were crying out for an odour-eating blanket – but the man with the mat *couldn't prove* it. He hadn't test-marketed the product. Furthermore, he was talking about television advertising – about spending money in what Doug Richard called 'a heroically inappropriate way' – without even knowing if the product was viable.

He was offered suggestions for test marketing. Simon Woodroffe – who thought the concept might actually work – proffered advice along the lines of an editorial in a local paper (these are fairly cheap), putting the product on sale in local shops and then monitoring sales. Rachel Elnaugh, who thought the idea was innovative but not unique enough, aired her concerns about him giving up his job in IT for it. All the Dragons concurred that the innovator had proved the concept in his mind – but nowhere else. 'It is,' finished Doug Richard, 'your number one responsibility to yourself and the investor to prove a concept.'

The inventor of the 'Stable Table' hadn't proved his concept either. A device to stabilise wobbly restaurant tables, it had the same fundamental flaws as the above pitch. There was no proof or indication that anyone wanted it and, furthermore, no clear indication that there was a problem to solve in the first place. Duncan Bannatyne acknowledged that there was a problem, but the solution came from on high because 'that's why God invented beer mats'.

No one, seriously, was convinced that there was a problem to solve, and the inventor of the gadget didn't have any statistics at hand to prove otherwise. Nor, seemingly, had he addressed *whose* problem it would be. Restaurant tables are the responsibility of the restaurant, not of the customer. Why target the latter to solve the problems of the former? Still, at least it seemed that the product was unique:

Hopeful entrepreneur: 'I've spent two years looking to see if there's any competition.'

Rachel Elnaugh: 'Gosh, that's really sad, isn't it?'

# BRANDING

Branding. Bit of a buzzword, this. It started being bandied around a lot in the 1980s, really took off (or should we say 'achieved brand recognition') during the next decade and is now the Holy Grail of consumerism. Get yourself a brand that people talk about and you're in business. Big business.

## BUT WHAT *IS* A BRAND?

Here's what it isn't. A brand isn't a product. It's not a logo or an advertising shout line or a slogan. Nor is it necessarily a company name. It's not exactly an identity either, because it's actually about perception. A brand is, basically, a memory. It's a word or, sometimes, phrase that doesn't belong to anyone else (see Intellectual Property Rights) and that, if successful, becomes firmly embedded in the minds of a target audience. And not just as a word. If you're a master of all things ending in 'ing' – marketing, targeting, positioning – then your brand will not only become instantly recognisable as itself, but as a word that encompasses the entire experience of doing business with you.

So you're not just selling an image – you're fostering a culture to support that image. A brand encapsulates your competitive advantage and building it isn't just about what you do – it's about what you do differently from everyone else.

**'A brand for a company is like a reputation for a person . . . You earn reputation by trying to do hard things well.'** Jeff Bezos, founder of Amazon.com

McDonald's is a brand. It's one of the world's most instantly recognisable brands. True, it only sells food and drink, but that's not just what it's about. Some people would say that's not *at all* what it's about – but that just emphasises the point. People who would never dream of setting foot in McDonald's have an image, lodged in their memories, of the brand.

That's one of the reasons why, once you've established a brand, it's vital not to veer off-message. McDonald's did it once by introducing a posh burger. It wasn't actually called a posh burger (its name was Arch DeLuxe), but that was the message. And it was the *wrong* message. McDonald's isn't posh. The burger was a disaster.

British Airways also had a calamitous episode with their brand. Regardless of whether or not it ever was 'the world's favourite airline' as their advertising strap line once claimed, it was pretty firmly identified as the flag-carrier for Britain. Literally – it flew the Union Flag. And then they messed about with the tail fins of the planes and painted over the flag with a variety of different designs. There's a well-known phrase that encapsulates complaints from middle-class, middle-England – 'Outraged from Tunbridge Wells'. Tunbridge Wells was *really* outraged about that. The airline seemed to be flying the flag for the *zeitgeist* – for the global village – and departing from its core message and identity. Its *Britishness*.

So branding is of critical importance. It has regularly made a guest appearance in the *Dragons' Den*, and will no doubt continue to do so. It's crucial for small businesses operating in a highly competitive market.

So how do you, with your small business, set about getting your target market to see you as the preferred choice? You have to build your brand.

## TAKING ON THE COMPETITION

The good news for budding entrepreneurs is that a competitive market can create a favourable climate for innovators. We're used to 'newness'; we rather welcome and applaud the small guys rushing in and taking the wind from the sails of corporate giants. The corporate giants themselves, of course, hate what they call 'disruptive innovations'. Often they can't cope with the threats they pose. Why? Because large organisations usually don't have an entrepreneurial culture; they don't keep their business models, strategies and services in a constant state of renewal or flux. They don't tend to engage their employees (sorry, 'colleagues') on a deep creative, wise and emotional level. They're often not interested in transformational change.

'Businessmen go down with their business because they like the old way so well they cannot bring themselves to change.' – Henry Ford

Complacency can kill a large company – even before it has realised it's complacent:

'Chains of habit are too light to be felt until they are too heavy to be broken.' – Warren Buffett

This is good news for you, the entrepreneur, who can zip in with your 'core differentiator' (or USP) and create a differentiated way of doing things in an already established market. Amazon, for example, created a differentiated way of buying books and, with it, one of the strongest brands on the planet. 'What we want,' said founder Jeff Bezos, 'is to be something completely new. There is no physical analogue for what Amazon.com is becoming.'

Lack of branding was one of the reasons why one *Dragons' Den* entrepreneur got such a roasting from the Dragons. The business idea was for a range of aromatherapy products. And the money sought was partly for the purpose of taking on a PR company to 'help build the brand and work on the packaging'. But, as Rachel Elnaugh put it: 'The market is *heaving* with aromatherapy products. What's different about yours?' None of the Dragons were swayed by the claim that all the products were organic, or even that they offered unique blends of oils and essences.

The basic problem was the lack of branding. In fairness to the entrepreneur, brand-building was one of the reasons why she had ventured into the *Dragons' Den* in the first place, but she didn't appear to have sorted out the brand basics. The Dragons couldn't get a handle on any differentiator; the packaging and the logo looked appropriate for the aromatherapy market, but it didn't shout 'Buy me as opposed to any other product'.

Without a core differentiator, without the building blocks of a brand, the product didn't look viable. Especially in a hugely competitive marketplace. Rachel Elnaugh pointed this out, only to receive the answer 'I'm not fazed by competition.' Rachel Elnaugh fired back with 'Well you should be. You should be!'

And so should you. While small companies can, as stated above, launch a sort of guerrilla assault on an established market, they can't do it without a very strong core mission, message and identity. Without a brand. But before you rush off to get another business loan (see Chapter Five), don't make the mistake of thinking, as the aromatherapy entrepreneur did, that you have to throw huge amounts of money at brand-building. She wanted £50,000, a hefty chunk of which was intended for this purpose. As Doug Richard asked: 'With fifty thousand pounds, how are you going to communicate to a broad market audience that your aromatherapy is different from others?'

The point is that £50,000 is peanuts for brand-building in this sort of business. It's an expensive exercise, sometimes needlessly so. One of the most common mistakes made by start-ups is to waste too much money at the early stages by doing the wrong things. Advertising, for instance. If you throw money into advertising your new product or service you may well be throwing it down the drain. Research indicates that most brands build slowly and that advertising them too soon and too widely does not pay off. For the small business, it's better and cheaper to build brand awareness by public relations and word of mouth. The latter – and this can be a *real* bonus for the small business – also spreads like wildfire through the Internet. While it would be a mistake to build your web site and then sit back and hope for money to pour in, it's common sense to enable people to find you through the World Wide Web. It's cheap as well.

## WHEN TO ENTER THE MARKET

The aromatherapy entrepreneur was given a thick ear for, among other things, trying to enter a market already awash with products. She was, the Dragons reckoned, trying to jump on the aromatherapy bandwagon after it had already departed. They certainly weren't convinced that their investment would increase, as she intimated, by a factor of ten within the next five years. And they felt that the market, if not exactly at saturation point, had ceased its rapid growth. And growth is one of the key factors you should be looking for when you're trying to enter that market.

By definition, a fast-growing market has lots of new buyers. It's much easier to target new buyers than to try to make customers switch from an established brand to which they have become loyal.

Furthermore, many of the customers in a new market will be risk-takers. They're already doing something new, therefore they'll be predisposed to the notion of trying something else new. Your product. Established markets, on the other hand, have established customers with established loyalties. As history has shown, it's very difficult to rock The Establishment.

The optimum moment to enter a market is when it's relatively new but not *brand* new (pun intended). If you get in *too* early what you may be doing is, in effect, rushing onto the playing field before the game has been invented. There will be nobody to see you play. Far worse, from your point of view, there will be nobody to *pay* to see you play.

On another occasion, the sum of £50,000 made an appearance on the *Dragons' Den* for advertising purposes (brand awareness is increasingly seen as the primary purpose of advertising). The creator of a new odour-eating dog mat was slammed for his plans to spend that sum of money on advertising the product on television. As you'll no doubt know, TV advertising is extraordinarily expensive. Additionally, as Rachel Elnaugh pointed out, 'Do you know how many advertising messages each of us receives each day? Three thousand.'

To sum up, brands have several different functions:

- They mark you out from the competition
- They help build relationships and strike an emotional chord
- They can foster credibility
- They help build a reputation and create loyalty
- They identify the product's fitness for its purpose

If there's one essential message to convey about brands, it's probably the concept of consistency. Brands should be communicated consistently through several different channels: the product itself, the services you provide, the packaging, your web site and your customer service. Branding should be communicated through your distribution facilities as well. Even if your 'distribution network' is actually a van. If you're sending out the message, for example, that whatever you're doing is clean, quick and reliable, your van should reflect this. A dirty, slow and old van is not consistent with the message. Nor, actually, is a white van. It is the 'Essex girl' of transport. Paint your van. It'll show you mean business. Because make no mistake – it doesn't matter how creative you are, it doesn't matter how wonderful your idea is, or how poised the market is to receive it if you don't know how to do business. In the words of Thomas Watson, founder of IBM: 'Business is a game, the best game in the world – if you know how to play it.' So start learning to play . . .

# FROM THE DRAGON'S MOUTH: RACHEL ELNAUGH

A former tax consultant for Arthur Andersen, Rachel Elnaugh started her company, Red Letter Days, 'on a shoestring' from her front room. Now worth some £25 million, the company is also the UK market leader in gift experiences. Many of the most prestigious names in British retail – Harrods, Selfridges, House of Fraser and Debenhams among them – sell Red Letter Day experiences, thrills such as driving a Ferrari, flying in a hot-air balloon or in a private jet. The company is considered a model business for a new wave of British entrepreneurs and Rachel herself, runner-up to the Veuve Clicquot Businesswoman of the Year in 2002, is in big demand as an after-dinner and motivational speaker. She is also, of course, the only female Dragon.

'When I was approached to appear in *Dragons' Den,* it struck me that it was a really interesting idea. On a personal as well as a professional level – I'd never made any angel investments before. It's actually proved to be a real eye-opener. From the show itself and the correspondence I've received as a result of appearing on it, it's really struck me how difficult it is to get funding. I didn't know just how hard it still is. I don't actually think we're that well-served by sources of funding and I don't think there's enough support in this country – particularly at the level of investments of under £1 million. Banks, in my experience, are completely risk-averse. I tried that route when I was setting-up Red Letter Days. I was rejected – and I was only trying to borrow £7,500! My bank manager said, "I really don't want to do that to you, Rachel." I think he'd already decided I was going to fail. And I was prepared to put my own property up as collateral. In the end, I got the money through friends and family.

I think my background has helped me a great deal in my business experience. I grew up with four brothers so I was used to dealing in a man's world. You could say it was a very competitive childhood! Also, if you grow up around business (we were raised above my father's shop), you inherit a very strong work ethic. Even so, I think I was pretty naive and vulnerable when I started out with Red Letter Days. The successful women I meet now are generally more assertive. But you quickly become strong, sort of Boadicea-like and, yes, I think you have to over-compensate if you're a woman in business. But there's a very fine line between being hard and being strong – and you don't want to cross it.

Possibly the most important element for success in business is instinct. There's really no substitute for it. And in the entrepreneurial world, I actually think having a professional qualification like an MBA can be a huge handicap. In one of the investments I made in the first series – the Snowbone – one of the guys has the formal education and the other has the entrepreneurial flair. To be honest, I think formal education often encourages you to go for the standard business model, and, if there were only one piece of advice I could give to entrepreneurs, it would be "dare to be different".

There's no substitute, either, for hard work. However different you are, the concept of hard work always applies. One thing I've noticed from *Dragons' Den* is that some people think being an entrepreneur is like turning on a tap: you have an idea and 'whoosh' the money starts to flow. It's not like that! It's one thing to have a great idea – it's quite another to make it happen. An awful lot of it is down to personal qualities, to a "can do" positive attitude and a strong work ethic. People with a "get-rich-quick" mentality are heading for a huge disappointment. It's very dangerous in business to start out with the idea of making money. It's not about taking. You've got to focus on what you can give people. Money flows from giving people what they want.

And the get-rich-quick people are generally not prepared for the hard work or for the fact that, in a way, it gets harder as you

become more successful. There's this Utopian vision of "success" – but there are problems at every stage of the game. As the business expands, so do the problems. You become successful, so you employ staff. That brings regulations and new personalities on board. Then there's the danger of over-expansion and the constant problems of cash flow and finances. The problems always expand.

One of the great things about *Dragons' Den* is that I've been learning myself. In becoming involved with other people's businesses I've had to practise the art of trying to help as much as possible without taking over. In a way it's like having children – to a large extent you've got to leave them to find their own way. My investment experience has also proved that business *always* boils down to people and their attitudes. It's those with the positive attitude and the strong work ethic who succeed.

Attitude has also been one of the most interesting things about the second series. In the first series, no one knew what to expect. But in the second, people knew what it was all about and were a little more polished. The trouble is that some of them also came across as rather patronising! They thought they knew us and the reasons why we make investments. But I don't make investments "because I'm a woman" and I don't like being told things like "I know you're looking for this . . . ". I'm looking for good ideas with strong potential. And people with the right attitude behind them.'

# Chapter Three

# BUSINESS ACUMEN

'It's not that difficult to start a
business and do extremely well'
Duncan Bannatyne

# 'I see no business individual or acumen in front of me to carry that product forward.' Peter Jones to a failed entrepreneur

The National Business Awards – the most coveted and high profile business awards in Britain – have a category for the 'Entrepreneur of the Year'. This is the one you want to win. (Dragon Duncan Bannatyne nearly did – he was a finalist in 2004.) The judges are looking for 'the most outstanding individual who can best demonstrate exceptional vision and leadership in the establishment and development of an owner-led business'. And their major criteria are:

- Clear identification of a market opportunity
- Innovation and growth
- Evidence of a strong financial performance in terms of sales and profit growth

The key words, as regards your business acumen, are 'financial performance'. You may have the best idea in the world but if you're financially illiterate then you'll succeed in turning it into a large overdraft instead of a profitable business. You may not even get to the overdraft stage because no one will lend you any money. Instead, you'll find yourself, quite literally, in a dragon's den – be it the office of a bank manager, venture capitalist, business angel or trade association – and realise that you've jumped straight into

the deep end and you can't swim. Here are a few real-life examples from *Dragons' Den*:

Doug Richard: 'So you're valuing a company that does not yet exist at £3 million? Doesn't that sound a bit rich?'
Budding entrepreneur: 'No, because it's got your interest.'
Doug Richard: 'No, actually. You've just lost my interest.'
Duncan Bannatyne: 'And mine.'

Rachel Elnaugh: 'How much revenue have you generated in the last twelve months?'
Budding entrepreneurs: 'Um . . . well . . . it's sort of minimal.'

Doug Richard: 'You will not make a 60–70 per cent net profit because very, very few businesses do. You have under-counted costs that you have not yet thought through. I would be happy – thrilled – to make 30 per cent profit.'
Simon Woodroffe: 'Why is it worth £1.5 million? What are the sales?'
Budding entrepreneur: 'Currently, we estimate them to be in the region of six figures, no problem. But we currently have none.'

Budding entrepreneur: 'I don't deal with the business side.'
Doug Richard: 'You do now.'

Budding entrepreneur: 'I'm not saying the contract is a contract . . . I might have used that terminology but . . .'. And so on.

No one is going to expect you to be a financial wizard, accounting genius or sales guru. But what everyone *will* expect is a strong basic grasp of where you are and what you're aiming for. There is no better way to do this than through a business plan. Sadly, and all too often, there is no better way to bore someone than to tell them how to write a business plan. This needn't be the case.

# BUSINESS PLANS

There are many guides to writing business plans around, in fact, far too many. The Internet is awash with them, umpteen books trumpet the secrets of the perfect plan and just about everyone you approach will have their own take on what to put in your plan. Some of these aids are good, others are fairly indifferent. However, there are really only a few things you need to know about business plans. The first one is:

## WHAT ARE THEY FOR?

Primarily, a business plan is for you, the entrepreneur, because it forces you to consider every aspect of the business. And that's why you, the entrepreneur, should write it. (Pay absolutely no attention to anyone who says that the skills required to write a business plan have anything to do with the skills required for running a successful business.) A business plan is a statement of intent; a realisation, on paper, of your product's viability, of your goals and missions, of the industry you're in, of your business strategy, as well as an analysis of the market and the competition.

There is no set format for a business plan. There is, however, the 'formal' business plan (the one described in all the guides) which is of interest only to banks and institutions. If you're approaching such institutions then you should write a formal plan. They are extremely sensible. But no matter who you are approaching, you should also write a second business plan, which is of interest only to you, and fill it with passion for your business.

Somewhere in between the two will be the sort of business plan to show to angels and Dragons. If you're going to pitch to them for financial backing then you should already have found out what sort of people they are. If they, like you, are true entrepreneurs, then one thing will be for sure: **They will hate formal, detailed business plans. They will regard them as empty, meaningless exercises, far removed from the reality of running a business.**

That doesn't mean you should write something totally off the wall. Rather, you should write something that's a **true** reflection of you and your intentions. It should have passion and personality. It should also have these crucial elements:

- A full financial model
- A marketing strategy, including competition and product positioning
- A breakdown of people and management (If you think you don't have people to manage, think again. You've got yourself.)
- A five-year outlook

The 'five-year' projection is an industry standard – no matter what the industry. There are some, however – entrepreneurial guru Mark McCormack of IMG Management was one of them – who would say that five years is way too long and that a two-year projection is a more realistic option.

The reality is that no **business plan ever comes true anyway**. Life doesn't work that way and, in fact, that's not the point of the plan. The real purpose is to demonstrate to investors that you've thought and planned and comprehended what might happen in your business. A business plan is nothing more than a prediction of how a business will do, based on a series of best guesses around finance, markets, management and the economy as a whole. The real goal is to demonstrate that you're an entrepreneur with a viable proposition and not a dreamer or a fantasist.

# 'The way to make God laugh is to show him your business plan.'
## Simon Woodroffe

## DOING IT BY THE BOOK

A formal business plan should – actually, must – begin with a summary. Not a summary of your business but of the plan itself, highlighting the key points. Exposing your plan to the light of the day (or the fire of a Dragon) may be your first entry into the marketplace and your first attempt to advertise yourself and your product. As such, it's subject to the rules of advertising – an initial impression will be formed in, if not exactly the blink of an eyelid, then somewhere between eight and forty seconds. That's all the time you've got. So think of the summary in terms of the blurb on the back of a business book: does it command attention with its initial proposition? (In this case, your business idea.) Is it interesting enough to make someone want to read on? What will the other person get from reading it? Will it be worth the effort? Will it repay the investment?

Think of your summary, then, as an expression of one of the most enduring principles of advertising – AIDA, or Attention, Interest, Desire, Action. You want to grab the attention of investors; make them interested in reading more; instil in them the desire to be part of what you're offering. If you've succeeded in doing that, they will then take action of their own volition. And that action is to invest in you.

In subsequent sections, your plan should go on to include all the relevant information on:

● The objectives, mission and viability of your business

● The industry you're operating in

● Your product. You should clearly define your USP (Unique Selling Point), why people should buy what you're producing and how you plan to develop it

● The market: including its size, trends, historical data and any market research you have undertaken. You should also identify your target customer base

● The competition, together with analysis of their products, strategies, service and customers

● Your own strategy and implementation, including marketing plans, operational requirements and sales targets

● Your current financial status, requirements and forecasts, to include cash flow and funding

These are the most crucial elements, but bear in mind, a business plan, no matter how formal, is a fluid document. Nothing is set in stone; there is no recipe for guaranteed success and no perfect template. And no matter how much research you have done and how much you think you may know about the people you are approaching, you are, at the end of the day, flying into the unknown. But your business plan may well turn out to be your parachute . . .

# THE ENTREPRENEURIAL ENVIRONMENT IN BRITAIN

The Government has an objective (yes, it does have many, but this is a realistic one) to make the UK the best place in the world to start and grow a business. On this front, many would say that it isn't doing too badly.

The 2003 survey (the most recent) by the Department of Trade and Industry (DTI), shows that Britain does indeed have a healthy and dynamic enterprise culture. The Small Business Service (SBS) Household Survey of Entrepreneurship found that 13 per cent of adults are already involved in entrepreneurial activity and that 11 per cent are thinking about it. Of those already involved, three-quarters run a business – or are self-employed – as a main activity and the rest do it as a sideline. If you're in the sideline department, don't go into the *Dragons' Den*. Several people who went there got their fingers burned by insisting on 'keeping the day job'. Remember that commitment thing we mentioned earlier.

Weirdly, while 93 per cent of adults admire people who start their own business (what on earth do the other 7 per cent think?), far fewer people would actively encourage people they know to become entrepreneurs. Only 64 per cent said they would encourage a friend or relative to start a business. In 2001 it was 76 per cent. So why has the number gone down? It's supposed to be easier to start a business now. In fact, it *is* easier.

The biggest problem is one of perception. It's fear. **The greatest single barrier to entrepreneurial activity is the challenge of getting finance for the business**. Yet all too often that barrier is a mental construct rather than a hard reality. According to the above survey, around three-quarters of small businesses seeking finance experienced little difficulty in obtaining it. Yes, it's harder to obtain finance for a business *idea* – especially from banks – yet there are a great many sources of alternative funding (see page 86).

The second greatest fear that deters budding entrepreneurs is **fear of getting into debt**. That's where your knowledge of your finances and your business plan comes in. All businesses have debts; it's being aware of them and having a long-term strategy to deal with them that counts.

As regards sources of funding for start-ups, most people approach the obvious choice – their bank. Mostly, they're turned down. Then, all too often, nothing else happens. Banks don't usually offer advice on how to seek funding elsewhere, and people don't always know where else to go.

# SOURCES OF FUNDING

Budding entrepreneur (who failed to bloom) to Evan Davis: 'Banks won't give you anything if you're a young entrepreneur.'

That same entrepreneur and her business partner elicited this remark from Simon Woodroffe: 'They've got an attitude that the world's unfair.'

Well, the world – and your bank manager – have generally got better things to do than wonder if they're treating you fairly or unfairly. They're getting on with their own business. In fact, they're not actually thinking about you at all. It's *you* that has to think about you. And *you* have to be fair to yourself. The best way to do that, as regards potential sources of funding, is to explore all the options.

If you think you've got a viable idea, do not under any circumstances just rush to your bank and ask for a loan. Apart from the fact that banks are expensive sources of finance, they're certainly not the best bet for a new venture.

Do a bit of research first. **In this country there are currently over 2,500 business grant schemes and £5 billion worth of development capital available annually.** That's a lot of money and a lot of people who would be prepared to listen to you. Furthermore, most grant schemes are for new businesses and not existing ones.

Start looking around (and see Chapter Five for more details on sources of funding).

# FINANCES

In *Dragons' Den*, as in real life, budding entrepreneurs often became unstuck when it came to finances. The age-old dichotomy between creativity and practicality (that left brain/right brain stuff again) reared its head on numerous occasions. Yes, it's often difficult for creative people to get to grips with the financial side of business but it's vital that they do. Shakespeare knew a thing or two about being creative, but he also knew that 'Words pay no debts'.

You need to know about balance sheets, profit and loss accounts (sometimes referred to as statements of operation but more commonly known as P & Ls) and cash flow statements. And you need to have researched every item on your proposed budget sheet. (Whatever your business, closely estimated costs can be obtained from trade associations, Business Link schemes and government guidelines.) You need to know, especially, about profit. Profit is actually extremely difficult to calculate, as its measurement is contingent on a variety of factors. It would be unrealistic, when entering somewhere like the *Dragons' Den*, to have all of these factors at your fingertips. But you absolutely *have* to know what your projected turnover is going to be – and you will certainly be lynched if you don't know the difference between gross profit and net profit. One hapless entrepreneur was pulled apart for just this reason. Having established that her projected revenue for her first year was £250,000, she proceeded to state that most of it would be net profit. This elicited the blunt response from Doug Richard that 'It is entirely impossible that you will have a net profit of £190,000 on £250,000 of sales.' She was, indeed, referring to gross profit – and there's a world of difference between the two.

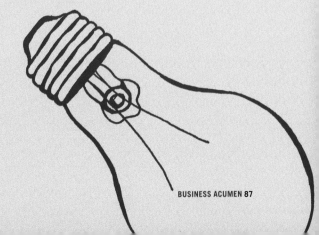

**'Money speaks sense in a language all nations understand.'**
Aphra Behn

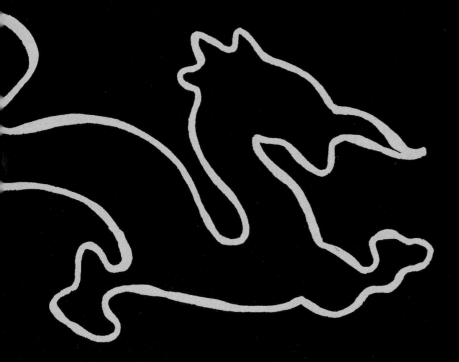

**Gross profit** is the actual direct profit made on a sale. It is the difference between the amount you bring in through sales (your turnover) minus the direct costs of that sale.

For example, if you sold a board game to a department store, your gross profit would be the revenue you receive from the store, minus the cost of producing the game itself.

**Net profit** is the gross profit, minus wages, overheads and depreciation. All these costs are inevitable when running a business, so your net profit is a better way of showing how profitable the business is overall. And as for overheads . . .

**Overheads** are expenses which cannot be directly charged against a product, division or invoiced sale. They normally include salaries, rent, printing, telecommunications, depreciation, advertising and promotion, etc.

You really need to get a grip on your overheads, projected or otherwise, because **overhead drift is a major cause of business failure**. Left to themselves, overhead costs drift only one way – upwards. They are the expenses of the business that don't vary directly with sales and, as such, they have to be extremely well-managed. They'll sink you if they soar out of control. Don't snatch a figure out of thin air and call it 'overheads'. Don't assume that overheads will increase by a certain percentage each year. Work it out. Start from a base of zero overheads. Everything above zero must be meticulously researched and accounted for. And keep looking at your overheads with an eye on eliminating costs that cannot be justified in terms of increasing sales, gross margin and net profit.

Another major cause of business failure is the **mismanagement of cash flow**. And cash flow is critical to the success of your business. Don't run out of money. You will not be able to pay your staff. Your staff will stop working for you. You will not be able

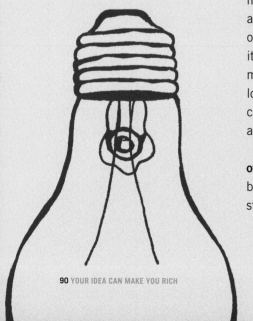

to pay your suppliers. They will stop supplying you. This is a simplistic way of putting it – but you get the picture. Your business will fail.

The most common reason for a small business to seek finance is for working capital/cash flow. (The second most common reason is for equipment and vehicles.) It isn't surprising: all businesses need cash reserves to keep afloat before sales reach break-even point. The old business adage 'cash is king' has never been so relevant than for the budding entrepreneur trying to hit the big time. Every business requires working capital as, inevitably, you will have to pay for supplies or fork out for wages before you get any money in from your customers. The wages part includes yourself, of course. Make sure you know exactly the amount you can afford to live on and include this in your calculations. Even if you've been used to a hefty salary in the past, you'll probably need to downscale your expectations in terms of income when you're starting off. In short, you'll need to have enough money in the bank to pay the bills while you wait for those cheques to arrive in the post. It's hardly surprising then that most businesses are looking for funding to make sure they are not caught short.

Interestingly, one of the most common reasons for entrepreneurs to enter the *Dragons' Den* was to seek money for marketing and advertising. Statistically, this is actually one of the least common reasons for small businesses and start-ups to seek finance. Maybe that's why most of the people who talked about advertising and marketing left the Den empty-handed . . .

Marketing a small and/or new business shouldn't, in any case, be expensive. After all, you're not planning to spend vast sums of cash on things like TV advertising, are you? If you are, you shouldn't be.

There are countless books, web sites and other resources available to those seeking financial and legal advice. This book isn't one of them. But it can point you in the right direction. And it seems that the best direction is often the one sign-posted 'accountant'.

The most consistently satisfactory advice for entrepreneurs and small businesses comes, surveys show, from an accountant. Trade and business associations rank almost as highly. Given that advice from an accountant will cost you money (although it will save you time), the associations affiliated with your business are probably the best port of call for a budding entrepreneur. There are other, highly-rated sources as well. Aspiring entrepreneurs should sharpen their business acumen by becoming acquainted with:

**Trade and business associations**
**Accountants**
**The Inland Revenue (www.hmrc.gov.uk)**
**The Internet**
**Libraries**
**The press**
**The Department of Trade and Industry (www.dti.gov.uk), The Small Business Service (www.sbs.gov.uk) and other government schemes such as Business Link (www.businesslink.gov.uk)**

One of the most common reasons cited by small businesses for not getting advice is 'not enough time'. But what are you doing if you don't make the time to seek advice and acquaint yourself with the facts and figures?

In their first year a third to a half of all new businesses fail
A third to half of all new businesses fail
Half of all new businesses fail
New businesses fail
businesses fail
fail

Many of us have heard that 'statistic' in the first line of the above. It's become something of a catchphrase, but more importantly, it's also become a deterrent. We know from Chapter One that failure can be a positive and a learning experience – but not if you reduce it down to one word. Sadly, that happens all too often. And it's not helped by the fact that most of the statistics that are bandied around are about businesses that fail. Why? Why don't we as a nation – and an entrepreneurial one at that – concentrate on success? So here's a statistic about success:

**The SBS Household Survey of Entrepreneurship found that 35 per cent of small businesses operating in 2003 had been started over ten years previously.**

That's pretty encouraging, isn't it?

# PROTECTING YOUR IDEAS

The protection of creativity, innovation and products all fall under the broad umbrella of Intellectual Property Rights. One of the (unsuccessful) budding entrepreneurs stated that her product was 'protected by Intellectual Property Rights worldwide' – a hugely sweeping remark. Either she was mistaken, or she had done a truly enormous amount of form filling. She would, in any case, have been better employed honing her presentation skills (see Chapter Four), because the Dragons didn't take kindly to her pitch. And that's putting it mildly . . .

Rights are essentially territorial, pertaining to specific countries or economic areas, and there are many different kinds of Intellectual Property (IP). For innovators and inventors, it's essential to know the basics. Broadly, IP is defined as creativity and innovation – ideas, if you like – and owning the rights to them means that, like physical property, they can be safeguarded. There are four main categories of IP:

## PATENTS

'I've invented the most amazing product. It's a . . . '

. . . Stop right there. Don't tell anyone what it is until you've patented it. Follow in the footsteps of Thomas Edison. He may be best remembered as the man who switched on the light bulb, but he was also awarded 1,368 patents during his lifetime. Your invention may or may not be the biggest thing since the light bulb, but until you've patented it you're unlikely to be credited with inventing it. It's a fact of life that if you're thinking of something 'new', then someone else probably will be too. Remember that synchronicity syndrome from Chapter One? It's also a fact of life that if your idea is a good one, then someone will try to rip it off.

Viewers of *Dragons' Den* will have seen that most of the people whose business idea was based on an invention or device had patented that device. In one instance – the special camera or IVCam patented by the Petty Brothers and invested in by Doug Richard and Peter Jones – the patent was reckoned to be worth as much as the investment, some £50,000. This is actually quite rare.

So how do patents work? A patent is granted by a country to an individual. It gives the grantee the right to prevent anyone else from making, using, selling or importing the patented invention for up to twenty years. In the case of the UK, patents have a long and noble history stretching back over 500 years. They can be applied for, and are filed at, the Patent Office. They also cost money (currently £30), so don't go rushing off to do a Thomas Edison.

That office should be one of your first ports of call when researching whether or not your invention is original – it has records of more than 30 million patents. But do try a fair amount of general research on the Internet first: you don't want to be trawling through the Patent Office web site if 'your' invention is already up and running and in the public domain. If you really feel you're onto something, you can also employ the services of a professional patent searcher or agent.

Remember that a patent is only valid in the country that has granted it. It's recommended that a patent should be obtained in the US as well as the UK, as most patent infringements appear to come from the US.

It should be noted that patents are a far from perfect way of protecting an invention or product. In *Dragons' Den*, two potential investors shied away from new products on the grounds that counterfeit copies would come and flood the market. One was a special 'grip' or sleeve for a football boot to facilitate expert kicking. It was kicked into touch by the Dragons, with one of them saying that as soon as it came onto the market there would be a flood of imitators from the Far East and elsewhere. This happens. It's also doubtful if an innovation like the above could anyway be patented. This is because a patent must involve an 'inventive step', and it's arguable if slipping a piece of clingy rubber over a football boot can be classed as such. Furthermore, the invention itself must take the practical form of an apparatus or device; a product such as some new material or substance, or an industrial process or method of operation. The SnowBone, a inventive snowboard attachment in which Rachel Elnaugh invested, had a good chance of getting a patent – yet Duncan

Bannatyne still had concerns about the design being copied.

The question of infringement and illegality is, unfortunately, a legal issue that can only be solved through extremely expensive court actions. In principle, something may be illegal; in practice, establishing that illegality and preventing a product hitting the market can be unenforceable.

But once you've been granted a patent on a product, you're free to talk about it. And, if you're seeking investment for developing it, you should. One budding entrepreneur – whose invention, a sort of personal air vehicle, captivated all the Dragons – said that he would rather not talk about the engine he had patented. Given that the engine contained all the secrets of the invention, this refusal to elaborate on its design stumped the Dragons – and they all pulled out. Reluctantly. Especially as they concurred that the little plane, or 'Flash Gordon device', would one day take to the skies. Just not with those particular Dragons in its wake.

## TRADEMARKS

A trademark is essentially your product's unique 'badge', comprising logos, colours, shapes and, in some cases, sounds, all of which differentiate your product from that of another manufacturer. It protects the use of the reputation that the mark represents. If a product is wearing a ® after its name, then you know it's a registered trademark. If it's accessorised with a ™ then it isn't necessarily registered but it is being used in a trademark *sense*.

It currently costs £200 to register a trademark in the UK, so you won't be registering any old name for fun. Huw Gwyther wasn't. He successfully trademarked the name of his aspirational, luxury magazine *Wonderland*, and secured a whopping investment of £175,000 from Peter Jones (although not, it has to be said, just for his *nous* in the trademark department). Anyone can use the word 'Wonderland' without infringing any rights: there are heaps of theme parks across the world bearing that name and Alice, after all, went to Wonderland long before Huw Gwyther was born. But no one else can now appropriate the word as the name of a magazine.

## DESIGN RIGHTS

The design of a product – the lines, contours, colours, shapes, textures and even materials – can be registered to give the owner protection. Without registration, the *rights* to the design still belong – automatically – to the owner. The process of registration, however, brings greater clarification of the legality of what can and cannot be done with these rights. In effect, registration helps build a stronger legal case against anyone copying designs.

## COPYRIGHT

Copyright gives the creators of literature, art, music and broadcasting control over their own output. Copyright applies as soon as there is a record of a work. It belongs automatically to the creator. There are no forms to fill in and no fees to pay. An extremely simple way of establishing your copyright of a design or a piece of writing is to mail it to yourself but to leave the envelope unopened. The postmark acts as proof of when the concept was generated.

# LICENSING

The right to a design can be bought, sold or, more commonly, licensed. So can the right to a copyright. Essentially, the owner of the rights controls the use of the work including whether, and how, to license it. So when one budding entrepreneur claimed that 'licensing is expected globally' she was – apart from revealing rather ambitious expectations – saying that, as the copyright owner, she was intending to sell rights for other companies to produce her product in other countries. She wasn't (and nor should you, unless you have a very good reason) granting anyone else an *exclusive* licence. Holding exclusive rights prevents anyone else, including you, the copyright owner, from having anything to do with the product.

Elizabeth Galton, the jewellery designer who succeeded in securing investment in the *Dragons' Den* (from Duncan Bannatyne and Rachel Elnaugh) had a brand that bore her own name. Duncan stated that the new company (to be created as a result of their investment) would 'own the rights to her name'. This doesn't mean that Elizabeth had given up her own name. It means that she would be entering into a legal agreement that meant she could not use her name for a rival business or retail venture if she ever left the company and that the company would retain the right to her name for the jewellery ranges. The precise details of the use of her name in a commercial context would, no doubt, have been hammered out at contract stage. But as regards the 'out' clause (also discussed), it would stipulate that Elizabeth herself could exit the company at some point in the future but that her name would stay. Her name, after all, is the brand.

For more information on all the above, including how to register your product, contact the UK Patent Office **(www.patent.gov.uk)**.

# EDUCATION IN BUSINESS AND ENTERPRISE

Only one successful entrepreneur in the *Dragon's Den* revealed that he had a business education. Paddy Radcliffe, the marketing man behind his partner Nick Rawcliffe's Snowbone snowboard attachment, had a degree in marketing and had worked in that environment for seven years. He had also just completed an MBA, the Holy Grail of business education. The letters stand for Master's in Business Administration and they carry a great deal of clout. Especially an MBA from a business school such as Stanford, Harvard, Yale, the London Business School or INSEAD. These are the blue chip big boys and they're very highly valued. The problem, nowadays, is that the University-of-Nowhere-in-

Particular-That-No-One-Has-Ever-Heard-Of is now offering MBAs and the currency has been devalued. Not only that, but the value of what's taught, even at the likes of Harvard, is now being questioned. The FT Executive Education 2005 Summary found that there is a rapidly increasing demand among corporations for customised programmes of business education. There is less of a desire to go with a business school such as Harvard, just because it is Harvard, and more of a drive to have programmes specifically tailored to a company's own needs. Something to think about when your company is up and running and ruling the world . . .

## AN ISSUE FOR DEBATE

The 2005 Annual Business Debate at the Oxford Union, the world's most famous debating society, proposed the motion that 'Management Education is not worth a bean'. Dragon Simon Woodroffe was the proposer; Sir Martin Sorrell, CEO of global advertising giant WPP and Deputy Chair of the London Business School, opposed the motion. Sorrell and Co. won. The motion was defeated. Resoundingly. The House concluded that Management Education is worth a bean. Several beans, in fact.

But there are still voices of dissent. There is, for example, the issue of corporate irresponsibility. Courses in the US that use as their model the excellence of Enron, you will be pleased to hear, have been rewritten. Corporate scandals and their deficit to society have, in fact, led a great many people to rethink what business and business education is actually all about. As regards the latter, some people were never in any doubt:

'All MBA graduates should have skulls and crossbones tattooed on their foreheads, along with warnings that they are not fit to manage. They are the products of schools that specialise in teaching the wrong things to the wrong people. Few MBA graduates have ever run anything and you cannot teach them to do so in a classroom.' – Henry Mintzberg, veteran US writer on management and management scholars.

Mintzberg (who is actually very highly regarded in the business world) also propounds the notion that trying to teach management to someone who has never managed is like trying to teach psychology to someone who has never met another human being.

Along with those who proposed and supported the motion at Oxford, Mintzberg belongs to the school of thought which argues that people studying for MBAs often don't understand what they're being educated *for*. Much of the teaching at business schools is heavily based on analysis. But as regards getting out and doing something, analysis can often lead to paralysis.

Simon Woodroffe is a passionate advocate of the imagination, something that he believes can be drummed out of us at school.

He says, 'I left school at sixteen. I honestly believe that part of the reason for my success is that I didn't have my imagination educated out of me.' In fact, he's even going back to the classroom to try and change the way business is 'taught': 'I'm involved in a really interesting charity called Edge,' he continues, 'that is trying to promote education by experience. The long term goal is to make a large percentage of the school curriculum experiential, to take pupils into the workplace; to also have people from the workplace come and share their experiences with pupils.

I challenge you to write two paragraphs about the Vikings. I bet you were educated about them at school, but unless you've been to a Viking ship or seen a Viking film I bet you can't remember much about them . . . '

There's a Chinese proverb that illustrates this perfectly:

*Tell me and I'll forget;*
*Show me and I may remember;*
*Involve me and I'll understand.*

Simon Woodroffe cites another potential MBA pitfall: 'They don't have a course in How to Fail, do they? They may well analyse classic business failures, but what you rarely read about is what happened to the people behind those failures. Many of them picked themselves up and started again. It's called being an entrepreneur . . . '.

'Ideas won't keep. Something must be done about them.' Alfred North Whitehead

Yet advocates of formal business education would argue that, while experience is a vital survival mechanism, it doesn't constitute a paradigm for learning. Experience, it has been said, is often about what to do or what not to do in certain situations, while remaining unaware of the theories that govern what you're trying to accomplish. An MBA will teach you those theories.

And, in purely financial terms, an MBA will reward you with more than theories. A two-year MBA course at a prestigious American University such as Harvard costs, on average, $130,000. Graduates can expect to increase their salaries by around $62,000 per annum in the first two years – effectively making the course pay for itself in a short space of time. MBA graduates from the London Business School can expect the qualification to pay for itself in around four years. And a survey from the Association of MBAs found that, in 2004, the average MBA graduate earned £65,000 p.a., plus £19,200 in variable cash earnings, such as performance-related bonuses. Not to be sniffed at. And having an MBA behind him helped Sir Martin Sorrell build a global advertising giant and earn, in 2004, £2.42 million. (That's actually the small stuff. He has shares in WPP worth about £90 million.) Maybe it taught him his debating skills as well . . .

Yet very few MBA graduates have jobs in sectors that actually *make* things. An MBA is pretty well essential, especially in America, if you're going to be a top-flight consultant or investment banker, but if your goal is to be a successful entrepreneur, the picture is far less clear. Most successful entrepreneurs don't have MBAs.

## 'Business schools reward difficult, complex behaviour more than simple behaviour, but simple behaviour is more effective.'
### Warren Buffett

And then there are the statistics from business schools themselves. Harvard's own research indicates that a very high percentage of their own 'entrepreneur' graduates are actually running small consultancies. Furthermore, very few businesses with high market capitalisation, both in the US and the UK, were founded by people with MBAs.

## BUT ARE THERE ANY STATISTICS ON THE CORRELATION BETWEEN EDUCATION AND ENTERPRISE?

Yes. The latest Small Business Service Survey of Entrepreneurship in the UK does demonstrate a relationship between level of education and entrepreneurial activity. It found that people with a degree (not an MBA) are more likely than average to be entrepreneurs (15 per cent compared to 13 per cent).

But what is really intriguing about the survey is that those actively involved in entrepreneurship are *less* likely than the population as a whole to have had any *enterprise* education: 53 per cent of entrepreneurs had no enterprise education, while 49 per cent of the population as a whole had no enterprise education.

So what's the answer as regards education and entrepreneurs? Lee Iacocca, former Chairman of Chrysler Corporation and one of the most widely recognised businessmen in the world, had a pretty good answer:

# 'Apply yourself. Get all the education you can but then, by God, do something. Don't just stand there. Make it happen.'

# FROM THE DRAGON'S MOUTH:
# SIMON WOODROFFE

After leaving school at the age of sixteen, Simon Woodroffe spent almost thirty years in the entertainment business. By the 1970s, his production companies were designing rock and roll stages for artists including Stevie Wonder, The Moody Blues and Rod Stewart. But, shortly after reaching the age of 40, he abruptly changed tack because 'inside I felt frustrated that I had never reached my full potential'. A Japanese acquaintance helped him realise that potential – he suggested Simon open a conveyor-belt sushi bar staffed by girls in black PVC miniskirts. The miniskirts never materialised but, in 1997, the first Yo! Sushi restaurant appeared. Two years later, with an ever-expanding business, Simon won the UK Entrepreneur of the Year Award. By 2003, there were seventeen Yo! Sushi restaurants and, in the same year, Simon sold a majority stake in the company, giving him the time and the capital to build other Yo! businesses, including the Yo! Japan clothing range and the forthcoming YOTEL! chain of hotels.

'There are lots of people who are unhappy in business and if
I can help them then the side benefits for all parties can be huge.
Approachability is my thing – that's also why I do a lot of public
speaking on entrepreneurship. I don't want my success to
separate me from the world, I want it to connect me. Also, it's
a lot of fun . . .

What I'm looking for in people and ideas is the "X Factor".
And someone who's not in denial; someone who has vision and
passion – but by no means someone who's completely blinded
by enthusiasm. I'm rather suspicious of someone who says they're
completely and utterly convinced beyond the shadow of a doubt
that their idea will succeed. Especially if it's risky. If there's one
thing that's absolutely true about successful entrepreneurs it's
that they're very, very careful about taking risks. If I'm using
other people's money I'm extremely careful about protecting it –
because I want more of it. Similarly, I don't want anyone to do
well at my expense: I want to be *with* them in their success.
There's no simple answer to the question of how to secure
funding for a business. Most people think the best way to get
investments out of people is to present a very good business plan
and tell the potential investor that they're going to make lots and

lots of money out of it. I don't think people succeed out of the greedy desire for money – it can't keep you going consistently for twelve or fourteen hours a day. But what *does* keep you going – it certainly keeps me going – is being fascinated by what you're doing. People don't invest in business just because they want to make money. There are other reasons. Sometimes *they* are the ones fascinated by what you're doing. Sometimes they don't want to be left out. Sometimes they don't want to turn down something that just might be successful. That's why investors need a lot of reassurance – and why the entrepreneur needs to be so committed.

I have this "seven meeting" rule. My experience is that if you've met someone that number of times, and if the experience has been good, then something will happen. So you have to be persistent with people. But don't badger them, and don't ask them for money. Don't try to get them to say "yes" – try to get them not to say "no". That way, when they show interest, *they* will be saying they want to invest in you. It won't be *you* asking them. So get people interested. Get them involved with what you're doing. But never ask them for too much and never put them under pressure.

Talking of pressure, I don't think our system of education is favourable to entrepreneurs. Kids are under so much pressure. It knocks the stuffing out of them and the school years are just the wrong time to be doing that. I really do believe that lots more children are going to come out of school wanting to start their own businesses, so they should be encouraged to feel they can

do anything. And that includes failing. Failure isn't encouraged in our culture. It just isn't acceptable. But what do most entrepreneurs do if they fail? They pick themselves up and they start again. You learn much more from failure than from success. I did. I thought we ruled the world when we opened Yo! Sushi, but then the failures started. We had to close several sites. The Bluewater site was in the wrong position, Edinburgh was too big . . . and then our Yo! Below bars failed. I was very disappointed. They had self-service beer, which no one had ever done before. And massage at the bar – how much closer can you get to your customers? We even had smoke-extracting ashtrays. But we didn't run the bars very well. We were a restaurant company and the bars distracted us from our core business. But we certainly learned lessons . . .

So my advice to entrepreneurs is to get out there and start failing. And to be mature with your emotions. You do need to touch people on a human level but you need to be emotionally mature enough not to let those people hurt you. And a sign of maturity is the realisation that life is difficult. Whatever happens – whatever anyone does and whatever difficulties you encounter – it is, in the end, down to you to deal with them. You can't change other people, but you *can* change your attitude towards them.

Oh, and another piece of advice I'd give to any entrepreneur is to throw away your TV. I know that sounds a bit odd coming from the *Dragons' Den*, but, believe me, you'll get a lot more done . . . '

'Presentation and packacking isn't just the 'fluffy' stuff to leave to the last minute . . . ' Peter Jones

# Chapter Four
# PITCHING AND PRESENTATION

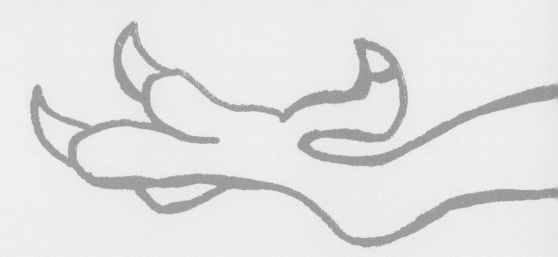

**Public speaking and presentation. They're second only to death in the fear ratings. Sometimes they're one and the same: death by public speaking. But if you're an entrepreneur you're going to have to get through the scary, nerve-racking process of pitching in public. You are the only person who knows your idea back-to-front and, if you're going to make it work, you have to sell it. That's what presentation is all about: selling yourself.**

In the wider business world, presentation methods are basically a foretaste of what a company's presentation culture will be. In the entrepreneurial environment, presentation methods are even more telling: they're a foretaste of what the whole company is going to be like. Because, at this stage, you *are* the company. How you present yourself, the words you use, how you express your idea, the clothes you wear, the figures you have in your head, how you respond to questions – they're all crucial. And it's far, far from being just about words. Some people believe that about 70 per cent of communication is actually non-verbal. Others have said it's 80 per cent and some have even stated that it's over 90 per cent. (It's also said that about 40 per cent of all statistics are actually made up, but let's ignore that.) The point is that what you actually say is only a small part of the story. People are going to make decisions that can make or break you based on how you present yourself. The importance of your pitching skills cannot be under-estimated.

Which is why *Dragons' Den* is such a superb platform from which to judge presentation skills. People who have seen the programme may well wonder how true to real life it was. Well . . . none of the presentations seen on television was rehearsed in front of cameras or the Dragons; the people who came up the stairs into the *Dragons' Den* were doing so for the first time, and none of them had ever met the Dragons before. Furthermore, none of the Dragons had been primed as to what they might be getting. They were in the Dragony Dark. So the programme actually exaggerates the rawness of the presentation process. But only in one sense does it depart from reality: it's the only pitching environment in the world where budding entrepreneurs will have ominous music played over them and then an interview with the BBC's Economics Editor to contend with. But, hey, it *is* television . . .

And people who appear on television are performing and that is *exactly* what you're doing when you're pitching an idea. You're not *putting on* a performance or acting a role. But you are, or should be, performing at your absolute best in order to give you and your idea the best chance of succeeding. And you're doing it under pressure. So how do you do it?

As with all aspects of business, there are shelves groaning under the weight of books telling you how to give the ideal presentation. Some of them are good and some of them are just awful. Hint: best to avoid the ones with exclamation marks all over the place – especially if they're in the title. This is about presenting, not exclaiming. Good presenters never exclaim.

But this is the only book that examines the performance of real-life budding entrepreneurs and, crucially, the way they were received by real investors. The lessons are culled from real life, not from theories. So here, from the investors themselves, are some of the cardinal rules:

**THE DRAGONS' TOP PITCHING TIPS:**

Doug Richard:
Understand what an investor is looking for

Duncan Bannatyne:
Know your numbers, know your percentages

Peter Jones:
Know your end goal and work towards it

Rachel Elnaugh:
Be passionate and objective about what you do

Simon Woodroffe:
Know the numbers instinctively – live and breathe them

**AND THE WORST PITCHING SINS:**

Doug Richard:
If it's too complicated to explain, it's too complex to understand

Duncan Bannatyne:
The worst thing you can ever do is to arrive late

Peter Jones:
Do not exaggerate the opportunity, be objective

Rachel Elnaugh:
Don't be pushy and arrogant

Simon Woodroffe:
Don't hide behind a veneer. We want to know who you are

# DOUG RICHARD'S PITCHER'S BIBLE

### THE PRODUCT

You have to be doing something unique. If you're opening a sandwich shop, remember there are a thousand other sandwich shops. What makes you different? If you can't say – in one single sentence – what makes you different, then you don't have a difference. Know what makes you different.

### THE IMPACT

You have to have a nose for opportunity. What's an opportunity? When you can sell to someone else and make a profit. So know the price of your product. Know the market that you're planning to sell it to. Have a way to prove all of this to the investor that you're pitching to. In doing this, you aim to show them that there is an opportunity and that you know the size of it. The size of the opportunity will translate directly, to that investor, the value of your company.

### THE INVESTOR

The first thing a person has to understand when pitching a business is what an investor is looking for. An investor is asking three questions:

- Is there a market?
- Is there an innovation?
- Is there something here that is different?

### PRESENTATION

If you're an entrepreneur and you're pitching, be aware that the investor is looking at how well you present, how well you dress, how well you carry yourself, how open you are to taking criticism and feedback. They're evaluating you as much as they're evaluating the company, the numbers and everything else that goes with it.

### THE STAKES

Know how much of the company you're prepared to sell before you walk in. If you don't know how much you want to give up, you won't know when to say 'yes' and when to say 'no'.

### THE PARTNERSHIP

Investors are not your enemies. Investors are your partners. When you sell a part of your company, what you're doing is getting married to a stranger for a very long time. Be prepared for that. If you don't like them from the outset then the chances are that you're not going to like them later. Even if you think you might get along with them, bear in mind that if you commit, you're committed for a long time.

# PREPARATION

But there's something you should do even before you get to the pitching stage. You should prepare. Then you should prepare again. And then again and again and again. Forget the fact that the *Dragons' Den* deliberately created and accentuated a nerve-racking environment. Whoever you're presenting to, whatever the room you're in, you're still going to be nervous. And if you're not, then *you should be*.

## RESEARCH YOUR AUDIENCE

You should already have found out as much as you can about the people you are presenting or pitching to. If you haven't, then you shouldn't be there in the first place. Similarly, familiarity with their own levels of expert knowledge is crucial – it's not much use blinding your audience with technical jargon if they only have a basic knowledge of your subject. Equally, a highly expert audience will soon switch off if you spend time plodding through the basics.

## COPING WITH NERVES

How to avoid the following:

'Oh dear ... oh dear ... let me start again. I'm going to start again in a minute ... I'll compose myself ...' – a budding entrepreneur pitching to the Dragons

If you are jangling with nerves before you go into the room, there are a few simple exercises you can do. Breathe very deeply and slowly for a few minutes and be aware of the release of your breath more than the intake. You are releasing your nerves. Scrunch up your fists into balls and then release – this has the same effect. Do similar exercises to tighten and release your leg muscles. Yawn to relax your throat. Speak out loud before you walk into the room to make sure your voice is ready to go.

The more dramatic the technique, the better. (The best presentation coaches have a background in drama.) To really get your voice going, shout or scream as loudly as you can. Then scream and shout even more loudly. Not only are you getting your voice ready but, more importantly, you are **releasing tension**. At the same time (you will have gathered by now that you need to be alone, preferably in a padded room, to do this), start dancing.

Not as if you're auditioning for *Come Dancing* – we're talking the full-on Ozzy Osbourne treatment here. This is the greatest gig you have ever been to and you are having a wild time.

In reality, it's highly unlikely that you're going to find yourself in an environment with a handy padded room on site. But this technique *works*. Try it at home when you're practising your presentation. On the day of the pitch itself, cast your mind back to that practice. What you're trying to do (and the breathing and muscle-clenching exercises should help) is access the feelings of confident relaxation, almost of elation, that you had after your jamming session. Take them with you into the room.

It's also a good idea to have someone video you when you're rehearsing your presentation. That way, you can actually see what you look and sound like when you're talking, and you'll be able to work on your body language beforehand. (You may well be rather embarrassed to find that some of your body language is best confined to the private anyway. People do the strangest things when they're talking. They scratch at the strangest places. Only by seeing yourself on tape can you be sure you aren't one of them.)

You may find that once you've dispensed with all that itching and scratching, handwaving and leaping about, you don't actually know what to *do* with yourself. Your hands really may have a mind of their own. With any luck, you'll have had an opportunity to case the joint before you pitch. If there's a table beside you or in front of you then use it. Hold on to it – but don't cling on for dear life. If you're going to be standing tall and straight then *stand* tall and straight. The best way to achieve a good posture is not to puff your chest out but to imagine that someone (God, probably – you may need him) is gently pulling you up from your crown. You'll stand taller and more confidently and, more importantly, you're making room for your diaphragm to expand and contract properly.

At the other end, be aware of your feet. Place them side by side and shoulder-width apart. Ground yourself. Feel that you're connecting properly to the earth beneath you. It will give you stability. Yes, of course you will move, but from this starting position, you'll move with confidence.

## WHY IT'S GOOD TO BE NERVOUS

We've all heard the most lauded and accomplished actors talking about stage fright; about jittering with nerves before going on stage. It always sounds a bit peculiar, doesn't it? Well, it isn't. The best public speakers and performers are always nervous beforehand because **they care about the reaction of the audience**. And they care about how the audience receives them. The latter point is critical: **communication is not, as is often taught, just about information given, it's more about information received**. That's why words only form part of the picture. As Alec Guinness said: 'An actor is totally vulnerable. His total personality is exposed to critical judgement – his intellect, his bearing, his diction, his whole appearance. In short, his ego.'

You, too, will be totally exposed during a presentation. So you have to develop and implement tools to cope with that exposure. The most basic one is learning your lines – you never hear actors saying that they didn't bother learning their lines and just went on stage hoping for the best. They know exactly what they're going to say. And so should you.

In the pitching environment, it's not a case of being word-perfect, but of knowing, if you like, the synopsis and not the script. Knowing the basics of what you're going to say and the order in which you're going to say it. Knowing the key facts and figures. That doesn't mean you should read from a script – you'd be booed off stage. But you can use prompt cards. And if you think you might be in danger of losing the plot then you *should* use them. Nobody will criticise you: using prompt cards shows you've thought about your presentation and prepared it properly. It's a good idea to take them along with you as security; you don't have to use the cards if you don't need to but they'll act as a vital back-up if your nerves get to you at the last minute.

Some entrepreneurs in the *Dragons' Den* did use them. Others should have. It would have saved them from making remarks like:

'I've got a cracking pitch. It was fine earlier but it's leaving me . . . '.

If you need prompt cards, however, to remind you of your opening salvo then you're in real trouble. It would mean that you can't remember your own name or that of your product/company. It's basic good manners to introduce yourself, to say why you're here and what you're offering. You should be able to do this succinctly. You don't want to ramble on forever and then have to face remarks like this (from Doug Richard):

'You've confused me comprehensively. What am I buying?' and 'I may have missed part of this, but what exactly happens at this event?'

You can be damn sure he didn't.

# VISUAL AIDS

There was a time when all IBM executives were expected to give their presentations using slides and overhead projectors. Failure to do so was seen as a sign of poor communication skills. Times have changed but, arguably, not enough.

Do not, under any circumstances, pitch your idea with the aid of a PowerPoint presentation. Even in the driest corners of the corporate world, there's an enormous backlash against them. It's called *Death by PowerPoint*: a long, dreary presentation in which someone pages through an on-screen presentation and reads slides aloud. Your audience will be very bored. Half of them will be very asleep. The people you are presenting to want to engage with *you*, your idea, your message, your passion, your business. Not with your computer.

Innovators have an advantage here in that, as seen in the *Dragons' Den*, they have something to show to their audience. Yet there are potential pitfalls here in that you don't want the focus to be exclusively on your invention. No matter what you're bringing into the room, don't place it centre stage and don't talk to it. Its function is to illustrate what you're saying. Let the interest in your product come from your audience, not from you. The best outcome is when they ask to be shown the product, or when they ask you to bring it closer. DO NOT HAND IT TO THEM AS YOU BEGIN YOUR PRESENTATION. True, one successful entrepreneur in the *Dragons' Den* did this, but it's not a cue you should follow. All human beings ignore you as soon as you put something in their hands. Even if you feel it's vital for them to read something as innocuous as a printed handout, tell them during the presentation that you'll hand it out afterwards. On the other hand, if they interrupt you mid-flow and ask to see what it is you're talking about, go ahead and give it to them. In the same vein, if you're interrupted by a question, do your best to answer it. **Always welcome questions from your audience.**

On one memorable occasion, Rachel Elnaugh asked an entrepreneur a question whilst he was in mid-flow. Not only was his response an irritated 'Just a sec', but his 'sec' lasted for about three minutes. The Dragons were already – and comprehensively – ripping apart the entire presentation, along with the proposition and personality behind it, but it was the treatment of Rachel Elnaugh that really got them going:

Rachel Elnaugh: 'What an obnoxious guy.'

Duncan Bannatyne to Rachel Elnaugh: 'On behalf of all men, I apologise for him.'

Rachel Elnaugh to the culprit: 'The most important thing for me in business is to work with people I like. I don't like you. You were rude to me and didn't come across as the sort of person I'd like to work with.'

The culprit to Evan Davis: 'She got the wrong end of the stick . . . she interrupted ME.'

He rather missed the point that a presentation should be a sophisticated, fluid and friendly conversation between buyer and seller.

# LANGUAGE, POSTURE AND DELIVERY

There are many techniques that can be used to improve your delivery of a presentation or pitch. Some of them should be obvious, but it's extraordinary how many people are oblivious to them. Here are a few:

- Maintain eye contact. It helps to build trust

- Don't slouch. It makes you look sloppy, not relaxed

- Don't fiddle with pens or bits of paper. It distracts your audience

- Don't move around too much. Your audience is trying to listen to what you're saying, not guess where you're going

- Use short, sharp and simple language – but try to keep as much spontaneity as you can. If you don't show any enthusiasm you can't expect your audience to have any either

- Even if you're talking to an expert audience, try not to use too many acronyms that are specific to your industry or business. You don't want to sound like a talking textbook

- Try to vary the volume, pitch and speed of delivery – but be aware that the average speed of delivery should be about three words per second

- Be aware that it's natural to speak more quickly when you're nervous. So be hopeful that your Ozzy Osborne performance has slowed you down

- Remember what Mae West said: 'An ounce of performance is worth pounds of promises.'

# DRESS

Some people can get away with anything. Most people can't. Unless your Technicolor Dreamcoat is an integral part of your personality then, please, leave it at home. Wear clothes smartly. Wear them politely. Wear them lightly.

People are going to form an initial impression of you and they're going to form it from your appearance. Of course they are. What else have they got to go on? They've never met you before. The impression is generally created subliminally – they're not usually consciously aware at this stage that they've already made a judgement about you. You want to keep it that way, but you want that judgement to create a favourable platform on which they will build other, acknowledged, judgements.

Most people only really notice what others are wearing if they're a) exceptionally beautifully dressed or b) look a complete fright. The vast majority of us fall somewhere in between. Unless – like several entrants into the *Dragons' Den* – your purpose is to advertise and launch your own brand of clothing or accessories (in which case you really need to make sure you belong to category a), it's best to keep it that way.

And don't make the mistake of thinking that just because your business idea has nothing to do with clothes then you shouldn't bother about them. Here's what Peter Jones said to the male occupant of an unironed shirt hanging over rumpled trousers:

'I think the way you've dressed today has done you absolutely no favours.' See? Clothes count.

# ATTITUDE

Aha. This is the clincher. The Dragons cited 'attitude' among their cardinal pitching sins. Being pushy and arrogant . . . exaggerating . . . hiding behind a veneer . . . You will not slay your Dragons with a dose of attitude.

There's a world of difference between having a healthy confidence in your idea and being convinced that everything you do and say is right. The former is attractive. The latter is arrogant. And arrogance is a deeply unattractive trait. Other people hate it – partly because it's a manifestation of an unwillingness to believe that you could ever be wrong.

Here are the sorts of reactions it provokes:

Duncan Bannatyne: 'I have come to the conclusion that you have this astonishing, absolutely amazing inability to listen to anybody.'

Rachel Elnaugh: 'You have this . . . sort of *arrogance.'*
Doug Richard (later): 'Arrogance, confidence . . . whatever
it is, it's complete obliviousness to what she faces.'

The point isn't just the arrogance. The whole attitude of
someone who engenders this kind of response is one of total
imperviousness to what anyone else says or thinks. It's the sort
of attitude that shouts I KNOW I AM RIGHT AND IF YOU
CRITICISE ME YOU ARE WRONG. The Dragons may well have
been wrong, but that's not the point. If someone offers you critical
advice – as they often were – in a pitching situation then you
acknowledge it. Graciously. As Simon Woodroffe says: 'One of
the greatest lessons I've learned is that criticism is much more
interesting than praise. And the most impressive reaction from
budding entrepreneurs is when you give them a criticism and
they take it on board, even acknowledge it with flattery. The best
sort of answer, along the lines of "you've really got a point there"
leaves the door open to you coming back into the conversation.
But someone who is in denial, who has complete blind faith in
their idea and won't listen to criticism . . . well, I'm highly
suspicious of that kind of attitude.'

Taking criticism on board doesn't mean you have to believe
it. You're perfectly entitled to walk out the door thinking,
as Woodroffe puts it, 'that advice was a load of old bollocks',
or you can accept it and build on it. Either way, don't be
personally affected by it. As Peter Jones said to one hapless
entrepreneur: 'I don't want you to take this personally, but I
think this is the most ludicrous thing I've ever seen.' Someone
else's opinion about you or your idea is just that – someone else's
opinion. Don't let it affect you. And don't, for heaven's sake, let
the people who have criticised you know that it has affected you.

# 'Nobody can make you feel inferior without your consent.'
## Eleanor Roosevelt

But that does not mean you should respond along the lines of:

'That's your opinion. That's good. That's your choice. From now on I'll address my questions and answers to those people who may be interested.'

The unsuccessful entrepreneur who offered that statement to one of the Dragons was probably feeling under pressure but, nonetheless, it shows the wrong attitude. Actually, it's just wrong. **If you're speaking to a panel, rather than a group of individual investors like the Dragons, then you continue speaking to the panel until you leave the room.** You don't cut anyone out because of something they said.

Nor, if you're seeking investment from someone, should you be defensive. Remember Doug Richard's advice that you are entering into a marriage? You don't want your intended to be asking you, as Rachel Elnaugh did to another entrepreneur, 'What's making you so defensive?' And you absolutely DON'T want to reply, 'Perhaps it's advice from my corporate lawyer . . . I don't want to disclose too much information.'

Unsurprisingly, the marriage – let alone the pre-nuptial agreement – was scuppered. The lesson is, don't throw your lawyer around until you get to contract stage. A pitch is your first date, and since when did anyone bring their lawyer along for the ride?

## PLAYING THE VICTIM

Do not do this. Do not project the attitude that life's unfair. Do not intimate that if you don't succeed with your pitch here and now your life and your business will fall apart. **Do not weep.** Peter Jones may have said that he found showing one's emotions demonstrated passion and determination but being a weeping woman in a roomful of men isn't, really, a very good idea. Rachel Elnaugh feels pretty strongly about it: 'I can tell you categorically that the biggest single turn-off in dealing with women in business is when they get emotional and tearful.'

## BEING OPEN AND HONEST

There are two parts to this: being honest about your product and your business (see Chapter Five), and being open about yourself. One of the Dragon's cardinal pitching sins is 'hiding behind a veneer'. The last thing you want to do is have someone saying:

'I'm not getting any sense of who you are. I can't connect with you.' – Simon Woodroffe

and 'Would I back the product? Possibly. Would I back you? No. You don't come across as very likeable.' – Rachel Elnaugh

The woman to whom these remarks were addressed may well have been the most likeable person in the world, but she wasn't being open. She was being cagey and defensive and, consequently, the Dragons found her unendearing and aggressive. You may know this by now and, if not, apologies for springing it on you, but **these people aren't real dragons**. They are your potential partners. They are also just people. That's right. Ordinary people. You really don't have to strive to keep them at bay. But the entrepreneur above seemed to be doing just that. 'No-one,' concluded Rachel Elnaugh, 'is going to back that woman. She has an attitude problem.'

# THE SUCCESSFUL PRESENTATIONS FROM THE *DRAGONS' DEN*

Here's a breakdown of the investment winners from the first series of *Dragons' Den*. These people were 'successful' in the sense that they achieved their investment goals. Don't forget, the offer is just the beginning of the story. It is followed by a process called 'due diligence' during which the business is scrutinised to ensure the investment opportunity has been accurately described. But would the pitching and presentation gurus trumpet the performances themselves as templates of perfection? Well, no, not really. Some

of the presentations were fabulous. Others were really dire. None of them, probably, went according to plan – and almost all of them broke 'rules' mentioned above. But, along with every other presentation ever known to mankind, they had one thing in common. People. And they demonstrated – successfully – that you cannot **ever** predict **anything** about other people.

## CHARLES EJOGU

Perhaps the best presentation took place in the very first episode of *Dragons' Den*. Charles Ejogu walked into the room carrying a photograph, which he immediately placed on the board beside him. Without taking his eyes off the Dragons, he proceeded to introduce himself and to state that he was here to seek £150,000 for investment in the world's first multimedia umbrella-vending machine: a unique product for a niche market. Then he pointed briefly to the photograph, enabling the Dragons to see that the vending machine was designed with a screen on the front to carry TV-style advertising.

Then came the information that he had secured exclusive rights from Cadbury Schweppes, who own sole vending rights to the London Underground, to install the machine in the network's stations; that the contract had twelve years to run; that there are over 300 stations – of which approximately half were viable in terms of passenger footfall figures and demographics for advertisers. In short, he added, that gave them access to 60–70 per cent of daily tube users – some two and a half million people – every day. The unit cost of the umbrella, he finished, was £2. The competition charged a minimum of £7. 'I think,' he concluded, 'I've covered everything.'

He had. He had spoken clearly and succinctly and had demonstrated:

- Exactly what his product was
- That it was indeed unique
- That it was viable
- That he had researched the market and the competition

It was pretty impressive. Then came the first spate of questions:

Where did you get the idea from?
What's your background?
What were the steps you took after first having the idea?

Charles, who had developed the idea after emerging from a tube station one rainy day without an umbrella, was an ex-investment banker with Merrill Lynch. He had been made redundant after two years. Take note: if you have been made redundant in the past then *say so*. Charles Ejogo gave the information in a matter-of-fact way because that's exactly what it is: matter of fact. Some budding entrepreneurs who had been made redundant tried to weasel away from the issue. Don't. You have nothing to be ashamed of. If you say you just 'left' your previous job then the question fired back at you will be 'Why?' If your answer isn't satisfactory it will begin to sow seeds of doubt. Potential investors may begin to suspect that something is amiss. And if you say something like 'the boss was difficult to work with' then they'll know something is definitely amiss. They may think *you* are difficult to work with and they're less likely to invest in you. As we've said before, be honest about yourself.

As regards the steps he took after developing the idea, Charles Ejogu was equally succinct. He said he had:

Found out if it had already been done
Designed the machine
Approached London Underground to get exclusive rights across the entire network, otherwise 'it would have been a complete waste of time'. The process of getting the contract, he said, took over a year.

Well, that speaks of a pretty high level of commitment to the idea, doesn't it? The Dragons, understandably, were rather impressed by the whole thing, especially as it was a two-fold idea: it satisfied a customer requirement (as Doug Richard said, 'I have huge confidence that it will rain in Britain') and it was also a potentially lucrative source of income as an advertising medium. One that Charles reckoned would generate twice as much revenue for the company as sales from the umbrella itself.

It was now pretty clear that Charles stood a good chance of securing investment. Ultimately, and after a great deal of negotiation over the equity he was offering – as well as an over-optimistic estimation of net profit* – he secured his investment from Peter Jones and Duncan Bannatyne. (A process that was not without its own little drama. Peter Jones to Duncan Bannatyne in mid-negotiation: 'You've been a sly little shit. I don't want to work with you.' See? Dragons are just like the rest of us.)

* 'You will not make 60–70 per cent net profit because very, very few businesses do. You have under-counted costs that you have not yet thought through. I would be happy – thrilled – to make 30 per cent.' – Doug Richard

Although Charles ended up selling twice the amount of equity (40 per cent as opposed to 20 per cent) that he had originally intended to sell, a deal was struck.

'I look forward to seeing you as Entrepreneur of the Year.' – Doug Richard

'That was a fantastic presentation.' – Peter Jones

## TRACEY GRAILY

Tracey Graily came up the stairs and immediately shook hands with all the Dragons. This, actually, was not a particularly good thing to do. Why? **Because the people she was pitching to were sitting down and she was standing up**. Psychologists would explain this in rather more professional terms, but this obviously well-intentioned action set up a whole 'power thing'. Forget the business angle, this is universal: we instinctively want to be on the same level as the person greeting us. Tracey Graily was inadvertently assuming a position of power over the Dragons. Dragons don't like this.

Not a great start, but rescued by the fact that Tracey went on to be clear and succinct about her business. It was a company geared to providing tailor-made clothes, especially suits, for professional high-earning females. But Tracey put the emphasis on another angle – on the company's *mission*, not its product (see Chapter Two): she emphasised that her company **makes life easier** for these women. This was a really smart thing to say. 'Our target market,' she continued, 'is thirty-plus, earning over £70,000 a year, working full-time – and life is not easy.'

This showed a shrewd understanding of her core values. Yes, her company (which was already up and running) made clothes but, more importantly, it was going to make life easier for women who needed to look good but who were strapped for time in the looking-good department. Her company would give them that time, coming to the office or the home to 'offer not just made-to-measure suits but a full consultation that offers style, colour and advice'.

She then went on to demonstrate her knowledge of the market. Suits and jackets alone, she said, constituted a market worth £1.5 billion. Yet the high street 'puts *all* of us, ladies and gentlemen, in standard sizes, although none of us are standard.' The £120,000 she was seeking was, she said, primarily for getting consultants out to customers. (Full marks for mentioning the gentlemen – that involvement thing – given that she was talking to four of them. Well . . . four men, anyway.)

Then she said she would like to bring in two models (waiting downstairs) in order to show them two items from her range. Unsurprisingly, it was Rachel Elnaugh who asked to examine the garments more closely. And she went straight to the point, or rather, the hem. Sloppy stitching would have sunk Tracey. Fortunately, the finish was top-quality.

The Dragons then had their say. The first question was about Tracey's background. It transpired that she had been in corporate life for fifteen years, working for Mothercare and Asda, and that she had already invested £90,000 of her own money in her product. She had put her money where her mouth was.

Then, from Rachel Elnaugh: 'You didn't finish telling us about Mothercare. Did you get fired?'

'No. I got made redundant.'

Rachel nodded. See? Don't skirt around the issue. There are more pressing things to talk about. Tailor-made skirts, for example.

To sum up, Tracey's pitch was good and so were her suits. Yet the subsequent talks nearly scuppered her, mainly because of the salary she was expecting for herself. Her words 'I don't come cheap' were bordering on the aggressive (see *Attitude* above). The point she was making was that she was good; unfortunately, she gave the impression she was greedy. Is greed good? Not when you're starting out as an entrepreneur.

Simon Woodroffe declined investment because of his unease at her salary level. Peter Jones just wasn't impressed by the enterprise. 'It's impossible for you to grow. Believe me.' And Duncan Bannatyne gave her some career advice. 'This product is not viable . . . I think you should pull the plug on it and get a job.'

Rachel Elnaugh, however, was extremely interested. And she had a great deal of empathy with Tracey. 'I really feel for you. I absolutely understand where you've been, what you've been through, the juggle that you're doing . . . ' She reckoned that Tracey really needed some good PR and 'although I hate to say it, a high-profile woman with high-profile contacts who can kick-start you'.

Empathy was also part of Doug Richard's imperative for investing. His own wife fell into the category of Tracey's target market. 'She would have dearly loved someone like you around when she was slaving away for a large law firm. I think you *do* have a viable business,' he continued. 'I think the potential in this marketplace is considerable.' Yet the equity she was offering in a risky business was a major sticking point. 'I only know of one mechanism to offset risk and that's to take increased equity.'

After some serious negotiation and a promise to re-evaluate her own remuneration, she eventually secured investment from Rachel Elnaugh and Doug Richard. And, like Charles Ejogu before her, Tracey ended up parting with 40 and not 20 per cent of her company.

# TRACIE HERRTAGE

Here's a pitch that defied most of the rules you'll ever read about. What it lacked in professionalism (quite a lot) it made up for in enthusiasm. Loads of it. What it lacked in market knowledge (practically everything) it made up for in innovation.

Tracie came bounding up the stairs carrying what appeared to be a large duvet. After introducing herself, giving the name of her product – 'Le Beanock'– and the amount of investment she was looking for, she proceeded to unwrap the mysteries of said Le Beanock. Given that it continued to look like a large duvet – only getting progressively more unwieldy, this was a novel strategy. But what carried her through was her charm and breezy manner as she chatted to the Dragons. And her lack of self-consciousness. Most of us, let's face it, would look, and feel, a bit daft unravelling a Le Beanock in front of a group of scary strangers. Explaining that Le Beanock, a cross between a bean bag and a hammock, had grown out of an idea for making cushions for her children, Tracie said she believed that, with the right marketing, her product could 'revolutionise the three-piece suite' and would appeal to students and first-time buyers.

It didn't seem to appeal to the Dragons. They were all looking a little bemused, if not downright dubious. Supplied with very little information from Tracey and no facts or figures, they started asking questions.

The first, about price, nearly killed the whole thing stone dead. At £995 the large version of Le Beanock seemed out of kilter with the suggested market. Yet Tracie was undeterred, countering that London loft-dwellers and their ilk, with City incomes to dispose of, would also buy it. Peter Jones wasn't convinced. He called Le Beanock a 'hanging basket' and told her that 'To be perfectly frank, I've never seen anything so ridiculous'. Duncan Bannatyne went one step further. 'I think you're wasting your money. I think you're wasting your time. I don't think this has any future whatsoever.'

Simon Woodroffe, however, thought Le Beanock was 'funky' and would sell. So did Doug Richard – although he finished up with: 'I'm not going to invest in you because I don't see a sufficiently large opportunity.'

Rachel Elnaugh was captivated. 'I have to say I think it's fabulous. And I think you're great.' In the end, she invested the £54,000 Tracie was seeking – although for a whopping 49 per cent equity (as opposed to the 30 per cent Tracie had intended to part with). The weaknesses of the pitch, and the fact that the concept was as yet unproven, were hurdles that could be overcome. 'At its heart,' said Rachel Elnaugh, 'it's a great concept.'

## THE PETTY BROTHERS

This presentation was really quite stunningly bad. The product behind it, however, was stunningly good.

Philip Petty needed a flapping A4 sheet of paper (tip: use discreetly sized cue cards if you need prompting) from the very beginning, but he was crippled by nerves before he'd even begun. He made several false starts: 'I'm here today to introduce you to a new industrial system for measurement for . . . We've developed a camera . . . We've identified . . . We have made a camera that can take two- or three-dimensional images and can create two- or three-dimensional drawings on computer . . . '.

Having at last managed to tell the Dragons what he was trying to pitch to them, he then talked about the investment he and his brother John had already put into the idea, and the amount he was looking for. He finished with the words 'I hope I've identified all the points I've tried to identify. Any questions?'

Well . . . yes, there were. Most of the Dragons were completely stumped. Duncan Bannatyne, a self-confessed technophobe, asked if Philip could explain 'step by step, in simple language, how the camera worked'. He couldn't. Nor could his brother John, who had now joined him in the Den.

It didn't actually matter. What did matter was that both Peter Jones and Doug Richard had immediately identified a USP.

The Petty brothers had developed a completely original, highly marketable device with a wide variety of industrial applications. They had also patented it. Their problem, as they both freely admitted, was that they were out of their depth. They were engineers, not businessmen, and what they really needed was advice or, as Doug Richard put it, 'a really large quantity of business help'. Although the brothers had entered the Den wanting £50,000 in exchange for 5 per cent of equity in the company, Peter Jones and Doug Richard drove them up to 30 per cent.

Perhaps more accomplished negotiators, given such a saleable product, would have succeeded in giving up less equity? But the real point was that the brothers were stuck. They needed that help. And with Doug Richard's background in CAD tools and Peter Jones's expertise in product-to-market, they were going to get that help. That was the key to this presentation. Investment isn't just about money. It's also about mentors.

## PAUL THOMAS

Student Paul Thomas gave an extremely polished presentation, introducing himself, his company and its function with admirable clarity. The company was, he said, based on the production of black truffles – 'a form of underground mushroom that grows in conjunction with tree roots. Demand is so high,' he continued, 'that they command at wholesale price more per unit weight than is paid for gold. That's £1,000 per kilo based on last year's prices.

'Many people have tried to cultivate truffles,' he continued, 'but very few have succeeded. We've developed an enhanced technique, which means that with 2,500 trees we can expect a turnover in excess of £1 million in the next five to seven years. What we're asking for is £75,000 to buy land to set up this plantation. There's also the potential of a 10 per cent profit share, and if you take this, it will give you an income in excess of £100,000 per year.'

'In summary, the system represents an environmentally sound, financially secure and potentially very high-yielding investment, so thank you for listening.'

Well, that covered most bases, didn't it? Except the fundamental one. Paul Thomas had taken it for granted that his audience knew exactly what black truffles were for.

'Please excuse my absolute ignorance,' said Duncan Bannatyne, 'but I have to ask. What is a black truffle?'

A question that had the beneficial effect of provoking good-humoured banter among the Dragons and the presenter. Although the Dragons were deeply divided about the viability of the enterprise – not least because the system had yet to be proven – the investment was partly for the purchase of land. Always an attractive prospect. In the end, Simon Woodroffe agreed to invest. Rachel Elnaugh was interested as well, but Simon wanted to go in on his own with Paul Thomas. He didn't want company. 'You know what it's like,' he said to Rachel Elnaugh, 'with three in a bed.'

Best not to pursue that one any further.

## ELIZABETH GALTON

Another exceptionally accomplished presentation marked by a quality that no business coaching can teach. From the outset, Elizabeth Galton conveyed, without any demonstration of ego, the impression that she was going to succeed. She was confident without a trace of arrogance, friendly without being ingratiating and polished without being slick. She also knew her product and market inside out and back to front. And she had a highly impressive CV.

A fashion jeweller, she arrived with, and was wearing, her own highly distinctive creations. She had, she said, won major awards, received national press coverage, exhibited all over the world, was assistant jewellery editor of a high-end glossy, a graduate of the Royal College of Art and a lecturer at the Royal College of Fashion.

The Dragons all asked to see the pieces she'd brought. Not only that, they tried them on. The sight of four highly successful businessmen wearing enormous necklaces did a great deal for the already friendly atmosphere Elizabeth had created. There's an underlying psychology here. If the men hadn't already felt well-disposed towards Elizabeth, they would *never* have draped outsize jewellery around their necks – let alone be filmed doing so. Furthermore, after much discussion and humour about the enormity of the necklaces, it was Elizabeth herself who deftly turned the conversation to a more serious note. 'What we need to focus on,' she said, 'is that the products I'm looking to launch are small-scale versions of these.'

Then the questions began. Peter Jones asked her about her financial expectations, and if she had the figures in her head. She did. She talked of the gargantuan mark-ups in jewellery design – ranging from 145 to 1,482 per cent – especially when, after year two, her designs would be manufactured in China. (Note: these mark-ups did not take into account and placed no value on the arguably unquantifiable and certainly unique aspect of the business: Elizabeth's own qualifications, reputation, time and skill.)

But her business acumen was still under fire. Elizabeth breezed through all the questions, even looking faintly surprised that her commercial nous should be getting such a grilling. That's because she knew something we didn't. She would have been better-served had she announced it at the beginning of her pitch: **her designs sold. And they sold extremely well**. As a direct result of an advertisement in the *Financial Times*' 'How to Spend It' section (it's published every two weeks on Saturdays. It contains fabulous ideas about how to spend your fabulous money. You will want to read it soon), she had sold five couture pieces and made £30,000. That really got the Dragons interested.

In the end, both Duncan Bannatyne and Rachel Elnaugh agreed to invest £55,000 each. This would give Elizabeth the cash injection she needed to achieve her objective of producing smaller-scale pieces in large quantities at reasonable prices. The other Dragons, while declining investment, were effusive in their praise, and cited their reasons for non-investment. 'I don't think,' said Peter Jones, 'you would benefit from having me with you as a partner. I don't think I'm going to add any value to it. But I think you're a fantastic person and I think you've done brilliantly today.'

It was the concept of adding value (see Chapter Five) that also deterred Doug Richard. 'I don't know anything about this business. It's pure risk for a "techie". I have huge admiration for you but I can't add the value to this business that I could to others.'

As ever in the *Dragons' Den*, Elizabeth Galton had to part with rather more of her company than she would have wanted (30 per cent as opposed to 20 per cent). Strangely, with such a viable product on her hands, she had made little attempt to negotiate. When questioned about this by Evan Davis, she appeared completely unfazed. 'I'm very passionate and would have made it in the end. I really need to move forward with this product *now*.' (She had already revealed that galleries in London and New York were crying out for the smaller-scale pieces). 'My imperative,' she finished, 'is to move forward.'

## NICK RAWCLIFFE AND PADDY RADCLIFFE

These fellows adopted a fairly high-risk presentation strategy. Nick started the proceedings by saying, 'I'd like to introduce Paddy. He's got a Master's degree in Marketing. He's worked for seven years in the marketing and communications industry, specialising in contemporary culture. He's just finished his MBA (see Chapter Three) from Cranfield School of Management.'

Paddy then took up the reins with 'I'm going to introduce Nick to you. He's got a Master's degree in Mechanical Engineering and a Master's in Design from the RCA. He's a multi-award-winning designer and serial inventor. He's got an eye for the big idea but his feet are very firmly on the ground as well . . . '.

'It's not every day,' continued Nick, 'that you get to be part of a new extreme sport, but today is a special day.' Then, turning to the contraption they had brought with them, and with mounting enthusiasm, he said, 'Let me introduce you to the Snowbone. Basically, it's an attachment for a snowboard which turns it into a snow-based BMX . . . '.

Eat your heart out, James Bond. This was the real-life motorbike on skis. The skiing Dragons were intrigued.

The non-skiing ones were rather alarmed.

They could all have been highly irritated by the double-act presentation if it had gone badly. Nick and Paddy passed the baton between them (and continued to do so throughout) in an easy, practised manner that, if wrongly executed or badly prepared, could have been disastrous. Other budding entrepreneurs had tried this tack and had failed miserably. It's *really* difficult to do this kind of double act without it being either stagey or a total flop. And the key to doing it is your relationship with the other person.

One of the advantages of doing it well is that it enables people to quickly get to know the different personalities and their different skill-sets. It's really a version of the 'hard-cop, soft-cop routine'. Furthermore, having a 'creative' personality and a 'business' personality who interact well enables both to emphasise their particular skills. Creative enthusiasm, for example, can become annoying rather than endearing if there isn't a business head to balance it out.

There's also a hidden psychology behind successfully introducing someone other than yourself. Your audience tends to pay more attention. They look at both people but they reserve judgement a) about the one being introduced because he isn't talking and b) about the introducer because they don't yet know about him. Done well, this technique creates positive feelings and a desire to know more. If it's badly executed, it looks smug, appears cringe-making and creates a desire to smack the people pitching to you.

The Dragons, however, thought this whole venture was rather risky. Only Rachel Elnaugh – again, for a great deal more equity than the entrepreneurs had planned – was finally prepared to join them in their venture. And the most important reason, she said, was 'They're really great guys. I really like them as people.'

## HUW GWYTHER

'I'm Huw Gwyther. I'm twenty-eight years old and I'm here today to present my business proposal to you for investing £175,000 in a new publishing company I'm in the process of setting up. The primary aim of the business is to produce and launch an imaginatively-positioned new publication into the UK consumer magazine market. The magazine will be called *Wonderland* and will be bi-monthly (six issues per year). What we aim to create is an important modern brand that will quickly become synonymous with good taste, style and originality.'

Huw then proceeded to talk more about the intended brand, the target market and the private equity he had already raised for his venture. A hugely ambitious venture.

'Of all the businesses in the whole wide world,' said Simon Woodroffe, 'you've chosen the highest risk. Launching a new magazine is the hardest thing you can do.' With a background in the music business, Simon Woodroffe was the only Dragon with first-hand knowledge of the media industry.

Huw Gwyther was undeterred. He had worked in magazine publishing in London and New York. He denied that he spent all his time going to smart parties – but, undeniably, he wouldn't have looked out of place at them. Nor, in fact, would he have looked out of place roaring down a mountain in Switzerland chasing James Bond on a Snowbone. No bad thing, this; if you're going to launch an upmarket glossy magazine, it helps to look the part.

After discussions about the cover price, the target market (which, unusually for magazines, was to be unisex) and the projected content of the magazine, the Dragons, although extremely impressed by the polished performance, still looked dubious.

The magazine was pretty smooth as well. Huw had handed out a dummy copy so that the Dragons could examine the cover, layout and design. The title, it was noted, had been trademarked (see Chapter Three). This man clearly meant business. But the risk of launching a new title, with the enormous attendant start-up costs and a fickle, unproven market, deterred them all.

Except Peter Jones. 'High risk appeals to me,' he announced. He offered Huw the £175,000 he was looking for. But, echoing Doug Richard's earlier words, he offset his risk by taking 44 per cent of equity in the magazine, considerably more than the 17.5 per cent Huw had initially offered. In doing this, Peter made the biggest single investment of the series.

## SO WHAT ARE THE LESSONS TO BE LEARNED FROM THE SUCCESSES OF THE *DRAGONS' DEN*?

The first is this: **There are no rules. There are only suggestions.** The suggestions – like the ones outlined earlier in this chapter – are there for a reason. They're tried and tested and they've proved to be effective for others. But, essentially, they're just maps. They can help get you to where you're going, but they can't tell you exactly what you'll find when you get there. The colour, the people, their mood, the atmosphere – they're all unpredictable. And no amount of advice can determine or define the elusive 'X'-factor that, when present, works its mysterious alchemy and just makes things 'click'. But something clicked for these people. And their presentations showed that:

- You can present chaotically and still end up a winner

- If your idea is sensationally good you can stumble through your pitch and still be a winner

- Investors are not just after the 'big deal'. Sure, they want to make money, but they often want to *help* you as well

- People are interested in other people. In three of the above examples, the first questions from the Dragons were about the people and not the product

- Investors dislike being told that you 'don't come cheap'

- People – even frightening Dragony people – like having conversations

- All men are different from each other and so are all women

- All people are highly unpredictable

- Just because someone doesn't bite at your idea doesn't mean it's bad. It may not suit their investment portfolio. They may have no knowledge of your market. They may decide they can't add value

- They may be wrong

- The statistics about the optimum age for entrepreneurs may be right. Two of the investment winners were just short of their twenty-ninth birthdays . . .

- Statistics are only statistics. All the other winners were different ages

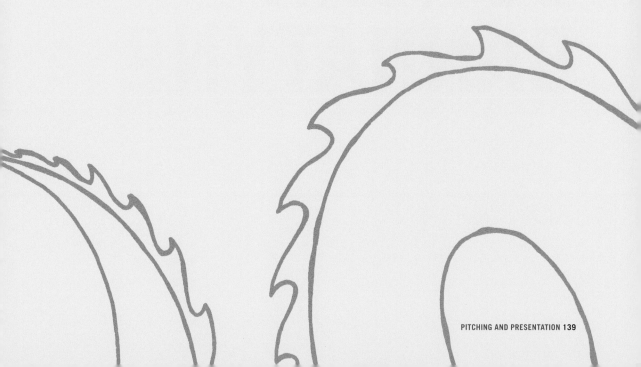

# FROM THE DRAGON'S MOUTH:
# DUNCAN BANNATYNE

Raised in Clydebank, Duncan joined – and left – the Navy while still in his teens. Moving to Stockton-on-Tees, he bought an ice cream van for £450. That van marked the arrival of a serial entrepreneur with a rapidly expanding fleet and a turnover of £300,000. After selling up, Duncan established Quality Care Nursing Homes and set up Just Learning children's day-care centres. A subsequent serious leg injury took him to a gym for the first time – an experience which led to Bannatyne's Fitness Ltd, a health club chain with a reported annual turnover of £30 million and more than thirty clubs. Duncan was Master Entrepreneur of the Year 2003 for the North Region and a finalist in the 2004 National Business Awards Entrepreneur of the Year. He has been awarded an OBE for services to business and charity.

'I thought doing *Dragons' Den* would be a great opportunity to make some investments. Then I quickly realised that it was a phenomenal way to broadcast the entrepreneurial message I've always wanted to tell. We don't *learn* about entrepreneurship; it's not taught in schools. What I really want people to know is that it's not that difficult to start a business and do extremely well. You don't have to do anything fantastic. It doesn't have to be about an invention. You don't have to have a good education or a degree – I don't! (But at the same time I want to make it clear that people should carry on with their education. It's free – and it's valuable.) But what you *do* have to have is self-belief, determination and drive. That's all. You really don't need anything else. Every other obstacle can be overcome.

On *Dragons' Den* we can tell – sometimes very quickly – who has got a chance of making it and who hasn't. If the product is completely unworkable, for instance, you've got a dreamer and not an entrepreneur. There have been quite a lot of those . . .

I've learned some things, too. I've learned – to my amazement – that people spend tens of thousands of pounds taking out worldwide patents and international copyrights and all the rest of it for ideas that are absolute rubbish. One lady from the first series (who didn't secure the Dragons' investment) said she'd spent *£60,000* on property rights . . . But, really, patents can be a complete waste of time unless you can quickly start manufacturing your product. Similar devices that don't breach your copyright can beat you to it.

I wish there were fewer inventions and more people coming in with business ideas. There *are* actually more people coming on the programme wanting to establish a business in the service industry. That's a good thing.

People still come on who aren't being completely honest. You can detect, really quickly, when people aren't being completely open. By that I mean telling the truth, the whole truth and all of the truth. If someone's keeping something back then I don't want to deal with them. I don't much want to deal with people who turn up late either. I'm always at least half an hour early for appointments.

Being an entrepreneur isn't, you know, about "being rich". That's not how it works. "Being rich" wasn't what happened to me. I first made money by selling ice creams; I wanted to make enough money to buy all my family members ice creams. We were poor – but we knew people who weren't poor and that's what I was striving towards. In the beginning, I didn't plan to have mega-wealth. I just wanted not to be poor. It all developed from that: I then wanted to carry on and make enough money to ensure that my children went to a nice school. What I then found out was that I was *enjoying* the business life and being an entrepreneur – so I kept doing it for the enjoyment. That's *much* more important than doing it for the money.

I think the entrepreneurial environment in this country is quite healthy. The main obstacles are mental ones, and people put them in the wrong place. A classic is, "It was easier in your day". Well, it *wasn't* easier in my day. I don't think it was more difficult either – I think it was probably exactly the same. What's different now is that there are more people from other countries who don't have English as a first language and who can't get executive jobs, so they set up on their own. I'm confident that there are people who are setting up businesses now, from practically nothing, that will be worth £100 or £200 million in ten years' time. It's happening now. Look at the Asian "Rich List". There are some people on it who don't have English as a first language and who started as entrepreneurs because they didn't fit into the system and, like me, didn't really have a choice.

So my message is quite simple. Anyone can build up a valuable business. You put your own obstacles in your way. It's not about having an invention and it doesn't have to be about being in the right place at the right time. With self-belief, determination and drive, anybody can do it. It's quite simple.'

'People don't invest in business just because they want to make money. There are other reasons.'
Simon Woodroffe

# Chapter Five
# INVESTORS

So you've done all your pitching preparation and you're ready to knock them dead with your masterful presentation skills. But, um . . . who are they? Who will be your Dragons? Where are you going to find them? And what sort of relationship do you want to have with them?

By living in the UK, you've already surmounted the first hurdle. You're in sunny climes as regards investment opportunities. As mentioned in Chapter Three, both public and private sectors in this country nurture the entrepreneurial spirit. And the options for investment are constantly increasing. Yet for most small businesses and budding entrepreneurs the bank is still the first port of call when seeking capital. There are good reasons for this, but none of them preclude you from casting your net wider. There are great shoals of financial fish swimming about – and very few of them are sharks. You just have to use your initiative to find them. And you *have* initiative. You used it to give birth to your great idea. Now you have to use it to give the idea its best chance of survival.

Broadly, there are two species of finance that you can raise to keep your business afloat: loan finance and equity finance.

# LOAN FINANCE

## BANKS

In the 2003 Survey of Entrepreneurship, half of all businesses surveyed (51.6 per cent) said they had sought a bank loan. A fifth had sought an overdraft. Yes, it's difficult to raise either if you have no track record, but it isn't true that banks discriminate against young people, as a couple trying to secure capital for a clothes shop in Glasgow said to Evan Davis.

Banks give their customers enormous amounts of money. The catch is that they want it back, with interest. And they want to know that you're capable of paying it back. But they're banks and not deities. You do not have to pray at the altar of your bank. They're not infallible (they are, after all, businesses . . . ) and some have better track records than others. If you're going to secure funding from a bank then find out more about them. Banking is an intensely competitive business and, as with everything else in business, relationships are critical. Ask around before you go into a bank – solicit opinions and ask advice from friends, businesses in your local area and enterprise networks.

## BANK LOANS

A loan from a bank is almost always cheaper than an overdraft. That's one of the reasons why half of small businesses seeking finance have used this channel. The other reason is that loans, usually given for a set period of time and a specific purpose, are ideal for purchasing fixed assets. Yet few banks will provide unsecured loans. They'll want collateral, they'll want a guarantee that you can pay it back. That guarantee may have to be in the form of a personal asset such as your home. If you have no suitable collateral you may qualify for the Small Firms Loan Guarantee Scheme in which the Government will guarantee 70 per cent (possibly more if you're an established business) of the loan. Your interest repayments will be greater, but, hell, it's worth a go, isn't it? Contact the Department of Trade and Industry for details **(www.dti.gov.uk)**.

## BANK OVERDRAFTS

You'll probably pay even more interest if you take out an overdraft. Overdrafts are the quickest and most flexible form of borrowing from banks, but beware of using them for anything other than short-term finance. Don't fund a fixed asset through an overdraft: it will take a long time to repay. And don't, for heaven's sake, exceed your overdraft limit. Your bank will wallop you with the most enormous charges and interest will accrue by the nano-second. You may well have gone over your limit because a client

hasn't paid *you*, but that's just tough, quite frankly. You will
end up paying through the nose for every phone call made, letter
written and cheque returned. It may be unfair – but you can bet
your bottom dollar (but best not to as it's all you've got left) that
it's written in the small print.

The other problem with overdrafts is that they can generally
be recalled at any time. Be aware of this. For small businesses,
and particularly for start-ups, a bank's interest in your success
is generally limited to your successful ability to repay them.
True, one repaid loan agreement or overdraft means they'll be
better disposed to lend to you again, but the bottom line is that
your bank isn't your business partner. Banks, as someone once
said, lend you an umbrella when the sun is shining – but they
may well want it back when it starts to rain.

## CREDIT CARDS

Do not, *under any circumstances*, use a credit card for anything
other then a short-term transaction or equally short-term method
of raising finance (i.e. when you know beyond the shadow of
a doubt that you can repay the money within your period of
interest-free credit). Don't make cash withdrawals on your credit
card. Don't build up debts on credit cards – it's a sure fire way
to bankruptcy. And don't believe that iniquitous sentence on your
statement that informs you of the amount you have 'available to
spend'. You don't. It's not your money. It's actually an invitation
to slide into debt and it shouldn't be allowed.

## MONEY LENDERS AND CREDIT AGENCIES

If you're thinking about these options then you shouldn't be
thinking of starting a business. You can't be trusted with money.

# EQUITY INVESTMENT

From Doug Richard's *Pitcher's Bible*:

## 'Investors are not your enemies. Investors are your partners. When you sell a part of your company, what you're doing is getting married to a stranger for a very long time. Be prepared for that.'

Raising money through equity investment is what *Dragons' Den* is all about. It means exchanging a share in your company for a capital sum. Usually you will have to relinquish an element of control in the company as well. As the Pitcher's Bible also says, 'Know how much of the company you're prepared to sell before you walk in' (see *Negotiating*, page 158). You'll also find that investors will want to nurture you and your business. They'll probably want a large say in management or even management control. So do your homework, too, in the advice department. Are you good at taking advice? Do you want it? Do you need it? One of the universal truths about being human is that we tend not to be skilled in spotting what we need. We confuse it with 'want' – and they're entirely different. And one of the problems for budding entrepreneurs, encountered repeatedly in *Dragons' Den,* is that they were wary, as regards both finance and management, of 'giving too much away'. One unsuccessful pair, who nearly secured investment but then pulled out of the negotiating process, told Evan Davis that they did so because they didn't want to make the 'classic mistake' made by inventors, that is, 'giving their inventions away'. The word 'gift' doesn't exactly spring to mind when you're parting with 26.3 per cent of a golf bag company in exchange for £125,000. Or maybe it does. Were they looking a gift-horse in the mouth?

Abandon all notions of 'giving away' and think of what you're gaining. And don't walk into the *Dragons' Den* or any other investment environment spoiling for a fight. Nobody can rip you off without your consent. But don't expect something for nothing either. As Simon Woodroffe said to a pair of particularly wary entrepreneurs:

'I can see the route you're going down. You're precious about what you've got and it feels to me like you think everybody's about to take it away from you … I can see you losing the whole thing … you're going to be hanging on for the right deal and one day you'll have no deal. Somebody else is going to come along and do it. My advice to you would be to get real. Just get real. Get with some decent people and try to get beyond that thing of mistrusting anyone who's an investor …'.

After all, you're much better having a small part of something tangible than you are having 100 per cent of nothing.

The end goal of the equity investor isn't to crow about how they ripped you off. It's to achieve growth in the companies in which they invest, ideally resulting in the sale of the company or its flotation on the stock market. You may, in some very rare instances, come across someone who is prepared to invest in your company 'just for the hell of it'. They want to be part of something that's fun. Or they like you. Or they're bored and want to have a new interest. Or they just want to get rid of some money (equity investments such as those made in the *Dragons' Den* are tax-deductible). Behind the scenes they will have an accountant urging tax-efficient means of disposing of money. Giving it to you is more efficient than tearing it up. But don't bank on this being the investor's motive. You are likely to be disappointed. You are also likely to come across as rather dim.

The risk-assessment criteria of equity investors are different from those of debt providers. They are, broadly, based on how likely the business is to succeed in the long term rather than how likely you are to be able to pay your debts. And, crucially, equity investors are likely to **add value** to the business by bringing their valuable skills, contacts, knowledge and advice.

## ADDING VALUE

Business angels – we're giving Dragons a re-branding in this chapter – often prove to be the ideal partners because they can add not just monetary value but value in the context of advice, managerial expertise and knowledge of the product and/or market. Time is money and the ideal business angel will provide a balance of both. As Doug Richard pointed out to one entrepreneur: 'You cannot afford my time and you need a great deal of business advice.' So, in simplistic terms, the entrepreneur agreed to give him more equity as payment for his advice.

Adding value is often as much about investors' own interests as it is about their areas of expertise. Look at the investments Rachel Elnaugh made: she agreed to invest in Tracie Herrtage's Le Beanock, the Snowbone vehicle and Tracey Graily's clothing and grooming consultancy company. Now look at Rachel Elnaugh's own company, Red Letter Days. It's one of the leading gift experience companies. Would any extreme sport-loving bloke turn down the experience of careering down a mountain on a Snowbone? Would a well-groomed woman turn down the chance of a made-to-measure suit with styling advice thrown in?

Furthermore, for Rachel Elnaugh, first-hand knowledge of a market is high on the agenda. As she said to a couple in whose idea she declined to invest: 'For me to invest in something, I need to know a bit about the market . . . where it fits . . . just to get a mental hook.'

Peter Jones, on the other hand, said to Elizabeth Galton that she wouldn't benefit from having him as a partner as he could not add any value.

Although he was highly impressed with both her performance and her business, the jewellery business just didn't fit into his portfolio (his major business is the Phones International Group). Elizabeth Galton seemed to know exactly where she was going and how she was going to get there. Not much point in coming along for the ride if you're not interested in jewellery. And not, probably, much risk involved. Huw Gwyther's magazine, in which Peter Jones pledged the largest investment of the first series, was a high-risk venture and, as Peter Jones said to the budding media mogul, 'High risk appeals to me.' As does the business of getting a product to the market. 'Product to market is my game,' he said to the Petty Brothers of their IVCam. 'Evaluating where sales channels will be . . . how you're going to employ a management team and deploy sales people to get the product into the market.'

Equity investors fall into two basic categories: **venture capitalists and business angels**.

## BUSINESS ANGELS

Business angels (or Dragons) are high net-worth private individuals who are looking to invest in companies that are likely to achieve high growth. **They are a very under-utilised source of investment in this country.**

Typically, a business angel will invest between £10,000 and £250,000. Most initial investments made are under £75,000. Again, typically, they will be able to bring first-hand experience (and, as mentioned, provide hands-on experience) to your business environment. Also known as informal investors, and often only answerable to themselves, business angels are usually in a position to make decisions quickly. And personality – yours and theirs – is likely to be a telling factor in their investment decision. Angels may collaborate with other angels. They may also fall out with them on occasion.

The disadvantages of business angels are that they don't invest regularly and, because of the criteria above, they may not be right for you. They can also be difficult to find. One way is to try the *Dragons' Den* itself – it may be television and classed as entertainment (but do remember the 'entrepreneur as entertainer' definition in Chapter One . . . ), yet these investors are real angels with real money. Alternatively, you can find a whole host of angels at the British Business Angels Association. This is the new National Trade Association for the country's Business Angel Networks. There are networks of angels all over the place. You want to find them. You want to network with them.

Backed by the DTI, the BBAA provides advice and contacts for those seeking funds as well as those looking to invest. You should make it one of your first ports of call in seeking investment. **www.bbaa.org.uk**

## VENTURE CAPITALISTS

Venture capitalists usually make much larger investments than business angels (generally investing a minimum of £2 million). They don't often invest in start-ups, and they often expect a high level of return on investment within a specific time-frame. Their input tends to be more formal, more hands-off and highly strategic. While business angels are very likely to take a hands-on role in management, venture capitalists are more likely to take a seat on the board and shout at you if you can't manage. An involvement with venture capitalists also carries kudos – it's likely to increase your chances of securing more funding from other sources. Bear in mind that venture capitalists usually need some sort of track record before they will invest and that if time isn't on your side they're not your best bet. Securing finance from a venture capitalist is generally a long and complex process with which you'll need professional help. But the rewards could be *very* substantial.

Although the inventors of a radically new golf bag announced in the Dragons' Den that they had already secured an investment of £100,000 from a venture capitalist in exchange for 20 per cent equity in the company.

Venture capital is, in fact, a major source of investment in the UK. It actually accounts for nearly 40 per cent of the whole of the European private equity market. **It is very big business.** The British Venture Capitalist Association represents more than 165 private equity firms in the UK, who have, since 1983, invested over **£60 billion in more than 25,000 companies**. In doing so, it has, according to the Association itself 'helped thousands of entrepreneurs start up and expand their company, to buy into a business, to buy out a division of their parent company, and to turn around or revitalise their business.'

Have a look at The Regional Venture Capital Fund as well as the BVCA. It may be up your street – literally. It's regional. With the aim of funding the 'equity gap' at the lower end of the market, it has a specific remit to match private venture capital to smaller enterprises. Operating across England, it provides funds in amounts of up to half a million – 'small-scale' in the risk finance world.

**The British Venture Capital Association (BVCA) www.bvca.co.uk**

**The Regional Venture Capital Fund (RVCF) www.sbs.gov.uk (click on Venture Capital)**

# SOME SOURCES OF FUNDING FOR SMALL BUSINESSES

In the UK, there are, as mentioned, over 2,500 various grant and loan schemes for which entrepreneurs and small businesses may be eligible. One of the best sources of information for grants available at a national level is the Department of Trade and Industry (DTI), **www.dti.gov.uk.** A mine of information, it also provides a direct link to **www.businesslink.gov.uk** and a Grants and Support Directory (GSD). The directory has listings of 2,802 schemes (some of which provide advice and assistance rather than finance) at both local and national levels, as well as details of some private grant-providing organisations.

**The Department of Trade and Industry**
**Response Centre**
**1 Victoria Street**
**London SW1H 0ET**

**Tel: 020 7215 5000**

For budding entrepreneurs aged between 14 and 30, The Prince's Trust, **www.princes-trust.org.uk**, provides loans, grants and advice. Last year, the Trust's Business Start-up programme helped 12,793 young entrepreneurs.

**The Prince's Trust**
**18 Park Square East**
**London NW1 4LH**

**Tel: 020 7543 1234**

The British Chambers of Commerce, **www.britishchambers.org.uk,** is an umbrella body for a national network of local Chambers of Commerce, representing more than 100,000 businesses in all sectors of the economy. While not a source of funding (although it does make annual awards), it can help you establish connections with businesses in your area which have been through the start-up and fund-raising process.

**British Chambers of Commerce**
**65 Petty France**
**London SW1H 9EU**

**Tel: 020 7654 5800**

There are many useful websites relating to sources of funding. There are also many useless ones, so the usual web caveats (especially concerning the word 'free') apply. One of the most reliable sites is **www.smallbusiness.co.uk**. Not entirely impartial (it's sponsored by Lloyds TSB), it does, however, contain an impressive amount of funding information and links, including those to angel networks.

# NEGOTIATING

## 'It is difficult to negotiate where neither will trust.' Samuel Johnson

Everything is negotiable. That's because an element of negotiation applies to everything – in life as well as in business. And in the latter, the negotiating buck doesn't stop with equity shares, as seen in *Dragons' Den*. If you've got a potential investor interested in collaborating with you, you'll have to negotiate the nitty-gritty – and you don't want to be the nit. You'll have to be prepared to discuss key issues like respective responsibilities, growth targets, the investor's – and your – exit strategy, contracts, indemnities, how the investment relationship will be managed and exactly what involvement the investors will have in the company.

Negotiating is about much more than money. It is about your style. It's about your approach. It's about **you**. Some of the most memorable scenes from *Dragons' Den* involved people who weren't prepared to lay all their cards on the negotiating table, who were evasive, disingenuous or even downright untruthful. In one instance, a couple of budding entrepreneurs later revealed to Evan Davis that they had had no intention of negotiating in the first place. This is just stupid – there is no point in entering the business playing field if you're not prepared to give and take. Worse, total intractability doesn't display strength – it reveals only weakness. Potential investors are trying to work with you. If your stance on negotiating can be summed up in the word 'no' then that word will, in the end, be thrown back at you. If you cast suspicion upon them, they will be suspicious of you. If you reveal that you think they want the shirt off your back, they won't want you to reveal your shirt, your back, or anything more about you.

Got the picture? Good negotiators don't try to manipulate or trick other people into making unsatisfactory arrangements. They don't believe that negotiating is a competition. They do not believe that anyone should be sneaky or aggressive or smarmy. Their goal is not to get a better outcome than their 'opponent'. Good negotiators are well prepared; they don't talk about 'winners' and 'losers' and they don't hurl phrases like 'it's a generous offer' across the table.

If they do, you probably shouldn't be negotiating with them. You have an alternative – or you should have. You really don't want to be in a position of needing the deal so badly that you cannot walk away from it. The other side is not, hopefully, the only game in town. Take succour from the fact that at least two hopeful entrepreneurs who were turned down by all five investors in the first series of *Dragons' Den* eventually managed to secure investment elsewhere. One had been told she was naively entering a viciously competitive market where she would be eaten alive. The other presented appallingly, was accused of being untrustworthy and was sent away with a flea in his ear – yet went on to raise capital from an alternative source. So remember that you're in a position of strength, not weakness. You are offering something that other people want. (You are, aren't you? If not, why not?)

Good negotiators always talk about getting to a win/win situation: an outcome that translates into 'you win AND I win' as opposed to 'You win OR I win'. And good negotiators are also chameleons. Their attitude, demeanour, approach and posture mirrors that of the person or people they are negotiating with. What they are looking for is 'common ground', or, to use the trendier current phrase – 'shared outcomes'. That doesn't mean that the whole negotiation process is window-dressing on a 'split-the-difference' exercise. That approach does indeed have its place – but that place is generally in a Marrakesh souk when you're haggling over the price of a rug. It's not – or shouldn't be – the underlying expectation and psychology of two parties in a boardroom. Negotiation is a partnership, not a gladiatorial contest. It's also a skill that can be monitored and developed.

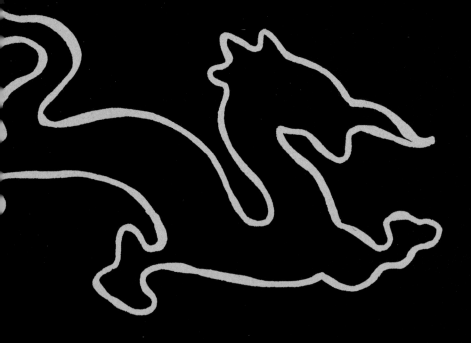

'Let us never negotiate out of fear. But let us never fear to negotiate.'
John F. Kennedy

There's a universally acclaimed exercise for developing negotiating skills called the 'Red/Blue Exercise'. You can find it on the Internet. It has spawned a noble lineage of negotiators.

So, too, have the following tips. Some of them will ring familiar bells. That's because they come with the prefix 'preparation'. As Henry Ford said: 'Before everything else, getting ready is the secret of success.'

If you're the one calling the meeting, choose an appropriate time and location for negotiation. Setting aside a few minutes for a chat in the car park is not ideal

Whoever calls the meeting, **prepare** for it. Then you should look back to the section on *Presentation* in Chapter Four. It tells you to prepare even more. Some 80 per cent of negotiation is about preparation and it's **vital**. And for goodness sake do, actually, be prepared to *negotiate*. One entrant into the *Dragons' Den* wasted everyone's time by offering concessions that he later retracted, ultimately declaring that he had never intended to move from his starting position anyway. That's not negotiating. It's called stringing people along. It leads to responses like 'I don't trust you' (Simon Woodroffe) and 'You've just lost the confidence of all five of us' (Rachel Elnaugh). These are not the sort of remarks you want bandied around, least of all on national television

Outline what you want from the negotiation and then identify the few – the *very few* – critical elements from the list. That means you should be distilling your list down to **'what is most important for me?'** NOT to **'here's everything I want'**

Do exactly the same for the person you're negotiating with. Amateurs often overlook this. Find out – as best you can – what the other person wants, why he or she wants it and what you think their most critical points will be. If you don't know the answers to these questions, you're not ready to negotiate. Do not pass go. Instead, go back and find out

While you're finding out, discover, too, what makes the other person or people tick. What are their motivations? What are their fears and anxieties? Are they trying to look good for their bosses or customers? And do they have personal problems, which may well be clouding their judgment? Remember: **everything that is part of or related to a deal has a value – and that includes emotional values**

When you've found out as much as you can about the other party, write it down. Put it beside the list of what you want. You're comparing, as it were, your shopping lists. If you see that you're both quite keen on asparagus, then asparagus is your common ground. You'll want to confirm your common ground early on in the proceedings. Hopefully you will both be able to grow asparagus on it

And while you're negotiating:

- Don't ever assume or deduce anything. Without sounding pedantic, confirm everything – both disagreement and disagreement

- Be prepared to concede on some important points in order to gain trust and get to the win/win outcome

- When asked something like 'Why will this be a fruitful venture for me?' don't respond with 'Good question' or 'Good question. Why will this be a fruitful venture for you?'. It shows that you're trying to buy time **because you are not prepared**. It also shows that you're not the best person with whom to forge an asparagus alliance

- Watch your language. Watch, in particular, the other person's language. Be ready to use other people's language as well as your own

- Call a spade a spade – not a tool to facilitate the manual excavation of topsoil. Don't mince words or hide disagreement, but **do** avoid inflaming emotion

- Similarly, don't shy away from your differences. You *will* disagree with the other party, but don't make a big deal of those differences. If you identify, specify and clarify them, you can then work on minimising them

- Don't beg. It's unseemly. More importantly, it will rob you of any deal or potential investment – and also your dignity. You may end up in the position of two girls who walked empty-handed out of the *Dragons' Den* escorted by the words 'you have an attitude that the world's unfair'.

- Consider the human factors. Take breaks. Get some air. Get some coffee. Let smokers nip out for a fag. You may find that you're all smokers, in which case you'll probably reach an extraordinarily amicable deal over a cigarette during those few minutes in the car park that you were advised against

- Don't bank on the above

- If you're going to cite 'legal advice' (as did one *Dragons' Den* hopeful) as a reason for not divulging information about yourself, for goodness sake bring your legal advisor with you

- Don't bring your legal advisor with you unless it's absolutely essential. Unless, for example, you're actually going to sign a contract at the meeting

- Have incremental goals. If the negotiations are complex or difficult, don't expect to resolve things in a single session

- Congratulate all parties on the progress you're making. Viewers of *Dragons' Den* will have seen the panel congratulate some of the entrepreneurs on their powers of negotiation. People like flattery. It's flattering. Here's Peter Jones to a pair of negotiators: 'I like your style of negotiation. You're not giving much away. I admire the tactic'. Unfortunately, the tactic backfired: the entrepreneurs continued not to give much away. In this they were highly successful: they left without having given or gained anything.

# CREATING THE RIGHT TEAM

If you've presented and negotiated successfully then you've proved your verbal dexterity, your business brain and your financial resolve. You've also proved something else – something that's going to serve you exceptionally well throughout your business career. You've proved your ability to communicate, to relate well to other people. It's arguably the most valuable tool in business. Because if you're going to go places, you'll be taking people with you. **You cannot do this on your own.** And not only will you be with other people all the way, you'll probably be managing them as well.

As you already know (because you've also proved your ability to digest the previous chapters), there is no relationship between being a great innovator and being a great businessperson or manager. Having an idea does not automatically confer on you the skills to manage others. Nor does having a business. But to have a successful business you *need* those skills. You need to be part of a team.

Entrepreneurs, by definition, are highly resourceful and highly motivated – and, by implication, highly individual. It's not surprising then that some of them baulk at the idea of being part of a team. After all, they took the entrepreneurial route and struck out 'on their own' precisely because they were sick to the back teeth of teams. Sick of team-building; sick of being frog-marched to corporate 'jollies'; of office politics and of being bombarded with bonding buzzwords. Sick, let's face it, of having to work with other people.

True, if you can't manage people, or don't want to, you may be in a position to get somebody else to do it. Plenty of people have entered the *Dragons' Den* in pairs; one person being the innovator and the other the business manager. That sort of relationship can, and in many cases does, continue after you've acquired capital, leading to a proper business partnership. Such partnerships work well where the roles are clearly defined but as your business grows you will, sooner or later, have a team around you.

But there are teams who consist of highly drilled automatons (the ones you wanted to smack) and there are teams comprising people who work loosely together, formally or informally, while travelling to the same destination. You want the latter sort of team around you. Call it a support network. You need it because having people on your side to call on – for whatever reason – is going to help you stay on the route to success.

Some of them are going to provide indispensable advice. In launching a start-up, for example, ideally you're going to need someone on your team who has start-up experience. Even if their company failed as a company, they can give you invaluable advice. If that sounds like a case of 'the blind leading the blind', then pause for a moment and ask yourself who, exactly, has the best qualifications to help someone with the experience of being blind? It's not someone with 20-20 vision, is it?

By all means take as much advice from as many quarters as you can, but be aware that start-ups are of a completely different order

**'No-one can possibly achieve any real or lasting success or "get rich" in business by being a conformist.'**
**John Paul Getty**

from other business experiences. Launching a company has little to do with working in a large corporation, a family business or with waving an MBA around. If you're lucky, your business angel may have earned his or her wings by soaring through a start-up. That's the person you want to fly with.

In starting a business, you have the enormous advantage – privilege, even – of establishing a culture. You, the entrepreneur, can create one that works. Well, you have to. You didn't, after all, inherit one.

Inheritance, in many large corporations, can be a burden. Strategies and hierarchical systems have often been set by people who no longer work for the company. And if they're still there they usually don't want to see them disrupted. The upside of this is the old adage 'If it ain't broke, don't fix it'. Things are ticking along quite nicely, thank you, so we don't want them tinkered with. The downside is insidious, potentially vast, and may well be the reason why you, the entrepreneur, left corporate life in the first place.

And what about happiness? Another study, conducted by the Forum for People Performance Management & Measurement at Northwestern University in the US, established a link between corporate profitability, satisfied customers – and happy employees. And the crucial element of contentment at work is **the way people derive happiness from groups**. Being part of a trusted, honest group is an indispensable part of contentment and engagement at work. Furthermore, the Forum's study (of 100 US media companies) showed that the small proportion of staff who dealt directly with the public **won't succeed unless the rest of the company is behind them**. There proved to be a direct link between the happiest and most engaged employees – across the company spectrum – and the highest-spending customers.

So what do many large corporations do about their teams? They leap on the voguish bandwagon of constantly disrupting them in order to provide them with new challenges and to achieve better results. So you left. To form your own company.

Of course it's easy to criticise large corporations. But the point is that when you're forming a company of your own, don't repeat the mistakes that may have caused you or your employees to become disenchanted with corporate life. One of those mistakes is to lose touch with your people. Another is to lose sight of your core values. And both of those mistakes arise, bizarrely, from the current trend to deny there is a problem to be solved, let alone a solution to seek, and that everyone is loved and everything is valued.

Who, for example, would cite 'passion for the world around us' as a core value? A Miss World contestant? No – it's Vodafone.

The Bank of America – currently ranked No. 10 in the FT Global 500 – doesn't fare much better. Here, in the words of its CEO, is its mission statement:

'The reason the Bank of America is in business is to help make communities stronger and help people achieve their dreams.'

Oh well, at least you know who to tap for that loan for the idea that will make you rich . . .

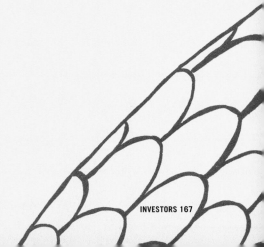

# FROM THE DRAGON'S MOUTH:
# PETER JONES

Peter Jones, the Chairman, CEO and founder of Phones International Group, knew he wanted to run a multi-million pound business as a schoolboy. And his childhood dream, which he had while sitting in the office of his father's Windsor-based air conditioning company, has certainly come true. Since its formation in April 1998, Phones International Group has experienced explosive growth and expects to generate revenues in excess of £200 million in 2005, delivering profits running into several millions. For Peter, this is just the latest in a long line of business achievements. At 28, he was appointed the youngest head of the PC business at computer firm Siemens Nixdorf, after having accelerated the company's UK sales of personal computers. His business acumen and strong head for figures revealed itself whilst he was still at school. At 16, after completing the Lawn Tennis Association's coaching examinations, he set up his own coaching school, combining the two school subjects he loved most and in which he excelled: sport and economics. In 2001, Peter was named by The Times newspaper and Ernst & Young as the Emerging Entrepreneur of the Year and, in 2003, Phones International Group was identified as the thirteenth fastest-growing business in The Sunday Times/Virgin Atlantic UK Fast Track League Table. It is now one of the most successful companies in the UK.

'I believe, very strongly, that I should add value to any business I am involved with. I review investment opportunities in the *Dragons' Den* based on the same criteria I use for anyone else who approaches me for help, advice and investment – and I get approached by scores of people. The key is, "Could I personally add value and make a real difference?" By the time I've got to that point, I've ticked the boxes asking if it interests me personally, if it's believable and realistic, what the likely return may be, and how much protection there is around the idea or invention.

Adding value could be on a very basic level in terms of contacts and networking, or knowledge and experience of a particular sector or discipline, but most importantly, it's about adding value to the top management – and that means "clicking" with the people driving the business. That doesn't mean we have to be best buddies, but it does mean there has to be something about the people involved that presses my buttons. And that "something" is usually to do with unwavering determination, self-belief, personal integrity and huge amounts of passion and enthusiasm.

Similarly, there has to be some sort of "X factor" in the marketing strategy and proposition of a new product. In *Dragons' Den*, I've been known to say that "product to market is my game" and it's been a recurring feature in my career to date, from my days in the PC industry through to mobile telecoms today. I relish challenging traditional norms and conventions, and I like to think I have a lot of value to add in the marketing strategy and proposition of a new product – particularly where the competition is active. That's where the "X factor" differentiation is required, and it's what I'm hot at: spotting the right angle and helping people to commercially exploit it to the maximum.

I'm also really hot on the need for entrepreneurs to invest in good presentation skills. It's a fact that in today's competitive business world you must make the effort to grab attention and make the right impact in order to win those precious minutes to make your pitch and get your idea across. Good ideas presented badly are a total failure. Presentation and packaging isn't just

the 'fluffy' stuff to leave to the last minute – it's integral to making you stand out from a very large and noisy crowd of wannabes. My advice to people entering the Dragons' Den is that, as well as making something look and sound good, it's also important to think about your audience, to match your message to the people you are presenting to. Badly-prepared people who don't know their stuff, or lack the passion and enthusiasm to drive their message home will always lose my interest.

And people will lose their business if they can't evaluate risk properly – it's a key area where many start-ups fall down. Some people who are true entrepreneurs, who are so highly-charged with self-belief and determination, will probably fly in the face of all risk, but, generally, it's a good idea to look at every possible way the rug can be pulled from under your feet. It will vary from situation to situation, but there are some key areas to consider as regards evaluating risk. Firstly, is the product/invention/idea protected? Lots of people fail to protect their ideas properly before engaging in communication with potential partners and customers, and they're aggrieved when someone takes their idea and does it for themselves. I don't advocate idea theft, but the onus is on the individuals with the ideas to protect themselves as much as possible.

But, in evaluating risk, I guess the area to focus most effort is in the financials. Are the people managing the finances up to the job? Have they covered every angle? What contingency measures are in place? Other things to consider include competitor strategies in the chosen market: how will existing players react and respond to new entrants? These factors only scrape the surface of risk evaluation – but they are key areas of focus for new entrepreneurs.

There's actually a huge demand for advice and investment in the UK. I hope *Dragons' Den* helps. On a more personal level, I'm also looking at developing some additional resources to try to help more people. I hope that in some small way, through my website **(www.petermeter.co.uk)** and through my other business activities, I'm doing my bit to help anyone who has a business goal.'

# Chapter Six
# YOU AND YOUR MONEY

'Anyone can build up a valuable business.' Duncan Bannatyne

# 'First get in, then get rich, then get respectable.' Bernie Ecclestone

So you've taken everything on board: you've done your research, got to grips with the financials, won that all-important investment and you are now the proud owner of a fledgling start-up. Well done. But don't go thinking you can sit back and take a break from all your hard work. This is only the beginning. Running a business is a huge undertaking and it is going to test – to the absolute limit – all of those skills you used to get it started in the first place. In fact, you'd need another whole book to cover this subject (and there are many excellent books out there which do just that). However, there is really no substitute for the gritty day-to-day experience of managing your own company, which, in the end, will be your most valuable and worthwhile lesson.

And, if you work extremely hard and the business begins to take off, you may end up as the proud recipient of one of those coveted Entrepreneur of the Year awards that Dragons like to display on their mantlepieces. Then, several more years down the line, you may find yourself at the helm of a prosperous and highly-respected company, managing an entire team of people (and that's another whole book). Your idea has, indeed, made you rich. Well, now may be the time to let your deputy – you'll have appointed one by now, of course – temporarily manage the business, while you take that exotic holiday you've been hankering after all these years.

But . . . even before you've packed your new Louis Vuitton cases, a thought may occur to you. There's something else that needs managing. Your money. Like it or not, if you're going to hang on to your money, you'll have to alter your itinerary. You're going to have to stop off at the wealth management industry. If you don't, you could be in for a nasty shock.

Let's imagine you don't, and instead you scamper off to the nearest yacht shop to buy the gin palace you've always hankered after. You have, say, a million in the bank. As rapidly becomes clear, a million pounds is peanuts in the yacht stakes, but you could easily downsize to a decent little number that will set you back £100,000. Well, you can easily afford that, can't you?

No, you can't. And here's why. With running costs and maintenance, your yacht is probably going to cost you somewhere in the region of £10,000 a year. Your investment income is now coming, not from the £1 million, but from the £900,000 you have in the bank. You can expect, net per annum (and this is being quite generous), a return of about 3.5 per cent from that amount. That's £31,500 a year. A third of which is going on the upkeep and running costs of your yacht. Not good, is it?

A million pounds is, actually, not very much. Millions of people have a million pounds. In this country, we have something in the region of 420,000 millionaires. It's no longer the exclusive club it once was.

And a million is not even a ripple in the ocean of the yacht/villa and Ferrari-owning classes. They certainly don't want you cluttering up the horizon with your poky little vessel. To be really rich nowadays, you need eight figures' worth of investable assets. And to get there, and stay there, you'll need people to help you. A lot of people. All of whom will want a cut of your money in return for managing your money.

Are you going to understand what any of them say? They'll be offering you a great deal of advice ranging from examples of 'wealth management workflow platforms' to 'holistic account aggregation' and – even more mind-boggling – the 'clearest single-window access to advice on best-of-breed products'. *What?*

No, having money does not necessarily make your life easier. It puts you into the premier league, but if you don't maintain your performance you can get demoted again. It puts you into the *Dragons' Den* – only this time you're sitting on the other side of the room beside a pile of money.

So what can you do with that money? Here are a few options:

## INVEST IN STOCKS AND SHARES

Very few people actually *become* very wealthy by investing in the stock market, but, with a well-balanced portfolio, it's a reliable, traditional and well-regulated vehicle for maintaining and increasing wealth. For the last ten years, the UK's stock exchange, the London Stock Exchange, has had a little brother who is growing up and becoming rather interesting. This is the AIM, or the Alternative Investment Market. Originally a market for small, young and growing companies, it was more often perceived as a home for poorly managed, risky companies. Now, however, its profile and performance have grown and it's become something of a hunting ground for investors looking to snap up smaller companies with big potential. True, some of the companies listed here are highly speculative but exciting investments can be made. And large sums of money *have* been made (and lost) by investors. Furthermore, there are, in some cases, significant tax benefits to be reaped from AIM as opposed to main market investments.

The other side of the coin is that, for successful entrepreneurs, a listing of your company on the AIM can provide you with an alternative source of funding to either banks or venture capitalists (see Chapter Five).

Yet investing in the stock market isn't a game for amateurs. If you don't know what you're doing, then don't do it. Get a stockbroker to advise you and do your trading. And be wary of one who tells you that you can make a quick fortune. If you're investing in the stock market you're basically doing one of two things: you're either looking for income (dividends) or capital growth (increase in share value). Either way you are seeking to preserve your wealth – not risk it.

Warren Buffett, however, famously made fortunes that way. Yet his advice was cautionary:

'I never attempt to make money on the stock market. I buy on the assumption that they could close the market the next day and not reopen it for five years.'

He also said:

'When a business does well, the stock eventually follows.'

So heed the words of an expert – you may eventually make big bucks from the stock market, but it's not the place for *fast* bucks.

## BECOME A BUSINESS ANGEL YOURSELF

Well, you know all about this now. And you know the basic principle of making investments in entrepreneurs. It's the same the world over. Even Donald Trump admits the principles are fairly basic: 'I know you're expecting sophisticated investment advice, but the wisest thing I can tell you is to invest only in products you understand, with people you know and trust.'

But beware of plunging vast amounts of your money into other people's businesses. Knowing what it means to be an entrepreneur isn't the same as actually running the show. The mechanics of this sort of investment are different: you're not in control and you're not there every day. Accountants Grant Thornton recommend setting aside no more than 15 per cent of your investment capital in risky, entrepreneurial ventures. They also advise caution in backing an entrepreneur who reminds you of yourself. They are not you. *You* are you.

## BECOME A PHILANTHROPIST

# 'There is no class so pitiably wretched as that which possesses money and nothing else.'
## Andrew Carnegie

That remark, a broadside at the yacht-dwelling classes, was made by the richest man on the planet at the time. In the nineteenth century, Andrew Carnegie, an immigrant from Scotland, made a fortune as an industrialist in the United States. In 1889 he wrote *The Gospel of Wealth*, in which he declared his belief that all personal wealth beyond what was needed to sustain one's family should be regarded as a trust fund to be administered for the benefit of the community. And he put his money where his mouth was. By the time of his death in 1919 he had given away in excess of $350 million. Most of it was for educational purposes, for he believed that 'Only in popular education can man erect the structure of an enduring civilisation.' Twelve Carnegie trusts continue his philanthropic work. The largest, The Carnegie Corporation of New York, is worth $1.9 billion and, in the last financial year, made grants of over $80 million.

In his day, Carnegie was the greatest philanthropist the world had ever seen. He started out as an entrepreneur.

So did Bill Gates. He had a computer thing going and it made him rich. Microsoft now has a capital valuation of over $262 billion. His company may not be ranked No. 1 in the world (it's currently third), but his charity is: The Bill and Melinda Gates Foundation is the world's largest charity, with an endowment worth almost $30 billion. Gates himself is reckoned to have donated even more, in real terms, than Andrew Carnegie. Makes you think, doesn't it?

The tradition continues closer to home. Duncan Bannatyne, who started life in a council flat, is now one of Britain's most successful entrepreneurs, worth over £130 million. In 2004 he was awarded an OBE – for services to charity.

## SPEND YOUR MONEY

Nobody's asking you to give everything away. Go on – splash out on yourself. You deserve it. Remember that *FT* supplement called 'How to Spend It?' Well, go on, buy it. It will only cost you £1.20 . . . But money isn't the point. If your idea really does make you rich, then you'll discover that true riches have very little to do with money. Lucre is a lovely sideline, but being really rich is actually a humbling experience, and it confers huge responsibility. It's not actually about you, anyway. Sam Walton knew this. He was an entrepreneur who had an idea for a little shop. He called it Wal-Mart. It's now the largest retailing corporation on the planet. And as Walton once said: 'The two most important words I ever wrote were on that first Wal-Mart sign: "Satisfaction Guaranteed!" They are still there.'

Becoming rich should be a satisfying experience: for you, for your friends and colleagues. It will help you build a better work environment, a better world – and a better life. So there's really quite a lot to be said for it, isn't there? Go for it . . .

If you would like to take your chances in the *Dragons' Den*, you can obtain an application form by sending your contact details to **dragonsden@bbc.co.uk**

# FURTHER READING

**How To Win Friends and Influence People**
Dale Carnegie
Vermilion
ISBN: 0749307846

The grandfather of all people-skills books was first published in 1937. It was an overnight hit, eventually selling 15 million copies. It's just as useful today, as Dale Carnegie's understanding of human nature will never be outdated. Financial success, Carnegie believed, is due 15 per cent to professional knowledge and 85 per cent to "the ability to express ideas, to assume leadership and to arouse enthusiasm among people."

**From Acorns . . . How to Build Your Brilliant Business From Scratch**
Caspian Woods
Prentice Hall
ISBN: 0273688057

In 2004, the *Sunday Times* reviewed this guide, saying 'There are other books that cover the same ground, but few that do so in such an entertaining and inspiring way.' That was before the publication of *Your Idea Can Make You Rich* which is, of course, infinitely more entertaining and much more inspiring.

**Anyone Can Do It: Building Coffee Republic From our Kitchen Table: 57 Real-Life laws on Entrepreneurship**
Sahar Hashemi, Bobby Hashemi
Capstone Publishing Ltd
ISBN: 1841125792

A good read for anyone put off by the 'this will never work' school of thought. It's also extremely illuminating as regards the enormous frustrations involved in starting a business. It details the staggering amounts of hard work and sheer determination (coupled with terror) required to pursue an idea – with no previous experience in the field – and make it a startling success.

**Good Small Business Guide:**
**How to Start and Grow Your Own Business**
Bloomsbury
Introduction by Martha Lane Fox
ISBN: 0747566909

Possibly the most comprehensive guide around at the moment.
It contains pretty well everything the entrepreneur would want
to know, and is particularly useful on the financial, legal and
administrative aspects of starting a business. It's not entertaining
(it's not meant to be) and can be quite hard work. But that's
a good thing. It makes it exactly like starting a business.

**Generation Entrepreneur**
Stuart Crainer, Des Dearlove
Financial Times Business
ISBN: 0273649205

Not so much a guide as a handbook for the new business
generation – the entrepreneurial, e-literate thirty-somethings
who have taken their lead from the likes of Michael Dell and
Jeff Bezos. It makes for inspirational reading – and leaves you
in no doubt that entrepreneurship is now a serious and viable
lifestyle choice.

**Venture Capital Handbook: An Entrepreneur's Guide**
Revised and Updated Edition
Financial Times/Prentice Hall
ISBN: 0130654930

A classic handbook on raising money to start a business, buy
a business, expand your existing one or invest in one. A practical
nuts-and-bolts guide to how VCs really work, it's also a fairly
comprehensive guide to the equity investment industry. It details
how to itemise what you want, how to get it, and who to approach.

**The British Library also offers a wealth of services for budding entrepreneurs.**

The Library is home to The **Business and Intellectual Property Centre** which offers arguably the largest collection of market research reports in the world, free access to on-line subscription databases giving up-to-the-minute company information and financial news, and access to the Library's extensive intellectual property resources, including its collection of 53 million patents, as well as a host of reference books and journals on a variety of business fields.

**Other useful services there, include:**

The **Product Novelty Service** which establishes whether a particular product idea is novel – very useful for finding out whether to apply for a patent for your idea, and

The **Library's Market Analysis Service** which is the ideal resource for those drawing up a business plan for their new venture: reference experts are on hand to search published information according to each user's requirements. In this way, entrepreneurs can establish whether a market is growing or contracting, who potential competitors might be, how their customer base breaks down, whether there are any other factors – such as impending legislation – that might affect the success of their business and whether or not grants or other forms of assistance are available.

# USEFUL WEBSITE ADDRESSES

## ESSENTIAL LINKS FOR BUSINESS INFORMATION:

**Business Link** – practical advice on all aspects of running
a business and how to finance it including information on equity
finance, the Enterprise Investment Scheme and how to find the
right investor
www.businesslink.gov.uk

**Start Talking Ideas** – help on how to develop your business ideas
www.starttalkingideas.org

**The Department of Trade and Industry**
www.dti.gov.uk

**The Chambers of Commerce**
www.chamberonline.co.uk

**The UK Patent Office**
www.patent.gov.uk

**The Business and Intellectual Property Centre**
www.bl.uk/services/reading/bipcentre.html

## AND FOR MORE TIPS AND INFORMATION
## FROM THE DRAGONS THEMSELVES, VISIT:

www.thegauntlet.com

www.petermeter.co.uk

www.rachelelnaugh.com

www.bbc.co.uk/dragonsden

# GLOSSARY

*AIM*
Alternative Investment Market

*angel investor*
High net-worth private individual who is looking to invest in companies that are likely to achieve high growth.

*balance sheet*
Statement which shows the assets and liabilities of a company on a particular date.

*brand*
Trademark, trade name, design etc., identifying a particular manufacturer's products.

*brand awareness*
Level of public familiarity with a branded product.

*business angel*
High net-worth private individual who is looking to invest in companies that are likely to achieve high growth.

*business plan*
A statement of business strategy including full financial model, product viability, analysis of market and competition, marketing strategy, breakdown of people and management, goals and mission and (usually) five-year outlook.

*capital growth*
Increase in value of investments.

*cash flow*
The movement of money in and out of a business.

*collateral*
Additional and separate security for repayment of money borrowed.

*copyright*
The sole right to reproduce a literary, dramatic, musical or artistic work, or to perform, translate, film or record such a work.

*core differentiator*
Unique selling point (USP)

*demographics*
The study of populations, especially in relation to size, density and distribution.

*design rights*
Ownership of the design of a product, including the lines, contours, colours, shapes, textures and even materials.

*dividend*
Income from stock market investments.

*entrepreneur*
One who undertakes an enterprise; one who owns and manages a business; a person who takes the risk of profit or loss. One who gets up entertainments.

*equity investment*
Business finance where a share of a company is exchanged for a capital sum.

*gross profit*
The actual amount brought in through sales minus the direct costs of those sales.

*indemnity*
Security from damage or loss.

*informal investors see business angels*

*intellectual property (IP)*
Property such as copyright, trademarks and patents, having no tangible form but representing the product of creative work or invention.

loan finance
Business finance in the form
of a loan which will be paid
back with interest.

market research
Research to determine
consumers' opinions about
a product or service.

marketing
The process of managing the
flow of goods, products or
services from the producer to
the user or consumer, involving
assessment of sales and
responsibility for promotion,
distribution and development.

marketplace
The world of commercial
transactions

MBA
Master of Business Administration

mentor
An experienced business person
appointed to help and advise a
less experienced business person.

mission statement
A statement of the benefit that
a company is offering and why
it is unique.

net profit
Gross profit minus wages,
overheads and depreciation.

overheads
Expenses which cannot be directly
charged against a product,
division
or invoiced sale. They normally
include salaries, rent, printing,
telecommunications,
depreciation, advertising and
promotion etc.

patent
An official document conferring
sole right for a term of years to the
proceeds of an invention.

profit see also gross profit;
net profit
Gain resulting from the use
of capital.

profit and loss account (P & L)
An account recording income and
expenditure, balanced, usually
annually, to show profits or losses.

statement of operation
Same as profit and loss account.

trademark
Any name or distinctive device
warranting goods for sale as
the production of any individual
or firm.

turnover
The money value of total sales
over a period.

USP
Unique selling point.

venture capital
Money supplied by individual
investors or business
organizations for new, especially
speculative, business enterprises.

working capital
Capital needed to carry on
a business.

# INDEX

## WITH THANKS TO...

Duncan Bannatyne, Rachel Elnaugh, Peter Jones, Theo Paphitis, Doug Richard, Simon Woodroffe, Evan Davis, the production team and crew of the BBC TWO series for all their hard work and to the producers John Hesling and Martyn Smith, the Executive Producer, David Tibballs and the Creative Head of Factual Entertainment, David Mortimer; Sharon Smith and Sabreena Peedoly at the BBC Commercial Agency, everyone at Smith & Gilmour, Graeme Grant, Amanda Li, Bob Richard, Christine King, Phyllis Van Reenan.